Twayne's United States Authors Series

Sylvia E. Bowman, *Editor*

INDIANA UNIVERSITY

Walter Van Tilburg Clark

Walter Van Tilburg Clark

By MAX WESTBROOK
University of Texas

 155

Twayne Publishers, Inc. :: New York

FOR FRANKIE LEA

Acknowledgments

Walter Clark has generously granted permission to quote from letters he has written to me.

The chapters on *The Ox-Bow Incident* and *The Watchful Gods* first appeared in *Western American Literature,* published at Colorado State University under the editorship of J. Golden Taylor.

I appreciate very much the kind permissions to quote from Clark's works as indicated by the following:

From *The Ox-Bow Incident,* by Walter Van Tilburg Clark. Copyright 1940 by Walter Van Tilburg Clark. Reprinted by permission of Random House, Inc.

From *The City of Trembling Leaves,* by Walter Van Tilburg Clark. Copyright 1945 by Walter Van Tilburg Clark. Reprinted by permission of Ashley Famous Agency, Inc.

From *The Track of the Cat,* by Walter Van Tilburg Clark. Copyright 1949 by Walter Van Tilburg Clark. Reprinted by permission of Random House, Inc.

Copyright 1950 by Walter Van Tilburg Clark. Reprinted from *The Watchful Gods and Other Stories,* by Walter Van Tilburg Clark, by permission of Random House, Inc.

Preface

When I wrote Walter Van Tilburg Clark telling him I planned to do a critical study of his work, his response was courteous and informative; but it began with a restrained demurrer. My project, though "flattering," contained a vague suggestion of the posthumous. He explained his feeling with an anecdote:

> Reminds me of a woman I was introduced to in the east. First just by name. Not too surprisingly, she didn't register. My hostess was determined to make a connection and said, "You know. Author of *The Ox-Bow Incident.*" Something very strange came into the lady's eyes—incredulity, calculation, revision, confusion. "You wrote that?" she asked. I admitted it. "You're *that* Clark?" she insisted. I admitted that. "My God," she burst out, "I thought you'd been dead for fifty years. You know, Owen Wister and all those people." [1]

The anecdote should not be taken as an unkindness to the lady, nor does it prove anything about Clark's reputation; but it points up graphically the type of question one feels to be irrelevant and yet, somehow, unavoidable. Even disciplined readers may find themselves interested in the fact that Stephen Crane wrote *The Red Badge of Courage* before he had seen combat; distractingly curious about the suicide of Ernest Hemingway; or, in Clark's case, puzzled by the fact that he has produced almost nothing of significance since 1950. Such questions seem unfair to the author, seem to invite easy-chair conjectures, sometimes smell slightly morbid, and certainly constitute an external approach to problems which, if legitimate, ought to be available for study in the literature itself. Still, though we may feel guilty for having come upon the question for suspicious reasons, there is often an uneasy feeling that the problem raised does have a legitimate, intrinsic existence. Thus we may snort righteously at men who raise the question and yet find our holy selves interested in deriving an answer. What *did* happen to Walter Van Tilburg Clark?

His first novel, *The Ox-Bow Incident* (1940), was a sudden success; and it is still considered perhaps the best of its genre. Clark's second novel, *The City of Trembling Leaves* (1945), about growing up in modern Reno, Nevada, disappointed most of its reviewers. In his third novel, *The Track of the Cat* (1949), Clark again used overtly Western materials (the setting is a Nevada ranch, 1900), although in a sophisticated and symbolical way. Reviewers gave him high praise for aiming at greatness, but many felt the novel had come shy of a satisfactory resolution. Since *The Watchful Gods* (1950), a collection of short fiction which received mixed reviews, Clark has been virtually silent.

Among leading critics of Western literature—like John R. Milton and the late Alan Swallow—Clark's reputation is secure. He is thought to be one of the best, perhaps *the* best, of Western writers; and his works, though few in number, are judged a significant achievement even apart from his role as Westerner, significant, that is, as literary art. In other parts of the country, however, Clark is largely forgotten, inaccurately remembered, or, at best, granted faint praise. *The Ox-Bow Incident* is sometimes mentioned favorably but usually in a negative way—as an exception, as a cowboy story which has literary merit in that it does not fall into the category of the horse opera. Readers who came along after the success of *The Ox-Bow Incident* often know Clark only as the author of "The Portable Phonograph," a minor and atypical but frequently anthologized short story.

None of these introductory remarks should be taken to mean that I consider Clark my cause célèbre. I do not consider him a major American novelist, nor do I consider it my duty to argue otherwise. Critics who turn partisan and exaggerate the worth of their subject commit a deceptive condescension and insult both themselves and their "man." Nor do I want to suggest anything pathetic about the career of Walter Clark. Alan Swallow's assessment of Clark's accomplishment, I think, is accurate: "what he has done has a permanent place, and many writers in a whole lifetime have not achieved more, or as much." [2] He has, in short, the high honor of having created at least three volumes of permanence, perhaps five; and thus envy, for all but a few, is an appropriate if ill-humored reaction. The most legitimate question about Clark's career, I think, will occur to anyone who reads his works carefully and then takes a look at the published reviews and criticism. Why has Clark been so consistently and so basically misread? And the answer to that question suggests—on intrinsic grounds—an insight into the awkward problem of his long silence.

When a novelist associated with a region writes with such talent that he lifts his works out of mere regionalism, reviewers in the forefront of the national literary scene seek to justify the artist's claim in terms already known on the national scene. This is what happened to Clark. *The Ox-Bow Incident,* coming out when the Nazi terror was strong and growing stronger, was taken by some as a parable of warning against fascism and thus as relevant to the nation. But this interpretation ignores the fact that no one in the novel uses Nazi techniques, believes in Nazi values, or works for Nazi aims. So excellent a critic as Edmund Wilson blundered with his review of *The City of Trembling Leaves,* chiding Clark for not making something—a marriage is suggested—of the relation between Tim Hazard and Rachel Wells. But if we read the novel in its own light and establish its context, we see that Clark *has* made something of the relation and that a marriage between Tim and Rachel would be as ill-conceived as marriage between Gatsby and Daisy. *The Track of the Cat,* despite high praise, has met a similar fate. Typical is the effort to use Melville's white whale as a means of explicating Clark's black painter, the discovery that this will not work, and then the astounding conclusion that *The Track of the Cat,* therefore, is not successfully resolved. Clark, to put it briefly, has been read in a preconceived context, and he has therefore been misread.

I am suspicious of make-up terms, which are so often words merely; but in Clark's case a new term is necessary. His values, as I understand them, simply have no name; and the fact that many schools of thought that do have names do turn out to be relevant to Clark proves to be more of a hindrance than a help. Clark is transcendentalist, for example, in that he emphasizes the necessity of thinking through concrete objects; and his interest in an ecstatic sense of unity with nature is suggestive of Whitman. But the German rationalism of early American transcendentalism is, for Clark, divisive rather than unitive and thus opposite to his own direction; Whitmanian ecstasy is handled by Clark with irony rather than with exhortation or celebration; and his concept of man and God (man's vicious animality and religious soul are equally fundamental; God is malevolent and indifferent as well as benevolent) calls for a dangerous type of unity that is antagonistic to the transcendentalist faith in correspondence. He is primitivist in his belief in the primordial, and comparable to D. H. Lawrence in his consistent portrayal of reason as a mechanism lacking in generative capability; yet his deep interest in the conscience and in rational morality constitutes a substantive barrier to either association. Images of atavism occur in Clark but as expressions of a psychological state, lacking ontological status. Oriental thought is important; but, like so many other American writers interested in the Orient, Clark is fascinated by problems of the one and the many, and seeks unity, yet breaks from the Oriental tradition with a democratic concern for the individual ego.

The established modes of thought most consistently held to by Clark are sacrality (as defined by Mircea Eliade in *The Sacred and the Profane*) and belief in the primacy of the unconscious mind (as explained by C. G. Jung in his famous essay on "Archetypes of the Collective Unconscious"). Both the unconscious and sacrality will be discussed throughout this book; but sacrality may briefly be defined as the belief that concrete acts, here and now, can recreate the primordial energy and meaning of the relevant cosmic or original act. A home, to use a typical illustration, represents for the sacred man the ordering of one's family under God; and the founding of the home is comparable to God's original act of bringing order out of chaos. To the profane man, a home may represent a financial investment or an effort to follow social conventions. To found a home in a sacred way is to tap primordial energies—within one's self and within the universe—and to relate the home to the real. To consider a home an investment is to serve profane values, to divide one's self from regenerative contact with the original.

Clark's belief in sacred unity is not to be confused with an escapist type of romanticism. He is stubbornly loyal to the profane efforts of American democracy, to that history which—however sacred or profane—is the history of the land and people he writes about. Thus the theme of sacrality is often handled with irony, for America's bold experiment in democracy makes awesome demands on the individual conscience. To move away from monarchy and aristocracy toward democracy is to emphasize the political and moral responsibility of the individual, his reasoned and therefore conscious responsibility. In religion, to move away from primitive ritual, the state-church, and priest-authority is to emphasize the responsibility of the individual. In the family, to de-emphasize predetermined roles is to increase the burden on individual creativity—if the family is to be anything other than a business arrangement. In economics, to stress initiative and a higher standard of living as the principles of political virtue is to leave the individual businessman and farmer with the task of finding something holy in his daily work, with the meaning of work limited to market values.

The irony of democracy—as Jung, Eliade, and others have pointed out—is that the responsible and free individual stands in a profane rather than a sacred relation to his world. If land is a means toward equal economic opportunity, then land is profane. If the father's authority over the son is only that authority which reason grants, then the relation of father to son is no longer holy. If the individual can choose his own religion, God can have no reality beyond the conscious reasoning through which the choice is made; if God is subject to man's reason, then God's superiority to man—indeed the very existence of God—becomes a pious wish of the intellect and is no longer a felt reality. If the ultimate authority for ethics is the vote of individual men, the ultimate meaning of our history cannot be greater than man's abilities in creation. The term I would like to suggest, then, is "American sacrality"—"sacrality" because Clark believes that the authoritative and archetypal voice of the unconscious has ontological status, and "American" because Clark believes that man has a paradoxical obligation to recognize his ethical role in American democracy. Man's duty is to unify his sacred self and his historical self.

Not many authors have faced this particular paradox as courageously as Walter Clark. The cowboy novelist (with one eye always on Hollywood) who flirts with this paradox often falls into nostalgia, diluting the sacred with sentimentality and ignoring altogether the irony of democracy. Major writers from other regions—and I intend no invidious comparison—have dared to move on different edges of the American paradox. Walt Whitman's poetry, for example, concentrates on exhortation and celebration rather than on the fact that a sacred man in a democracy must feel, through most of his practical day, totally absurd. J. D. Salinger is certainly concerned with sacrality, but the Glass family heroes have tortured themselves into a symbolic sacrality, a theme which is important to American culture and valid material for art. But the essence of sacrality is that the real is touched and felt, not symbolized or intellectualized through images of Christ as the Fat Lady; and this essence—as it still throbs in a people who worship the practical way of life—is Clark's chosen subject. John Steinbeck, if we restrict our comparison to the topic of boldness in facing both the sacred and the profane worlds, is probably closer to Clark than any other writer of national prominence.

Certainly, for Clark, to write without a sacred vision is to sell out to the narrow factualist; and to write without strict attention to the demands of the practical is to betray a fundamental duty of the writer. Yet to find and develop and unify materials which express both cosmological sacrality and the hard-level ironies of American democracy is incredibly difficult. Clark, it seems, has balked before his task; but, however truncated or interrupted his career may be, it represents one of the boldest efforts in American literary history, and it is an effort of considerable accomplishment. The chapters which follow, I hope, will help us to understand that accomplishment more accurately.

The first chapter includes a biographical sketch and concentrates on Clark's early writings and literary credo. The second, departing slightly from the custom of volumes in Twayne's United States Authors Series, is a discussion of Clark's place in Western literature. This chapter, because of widespread disagreements about the West and Western literature, seemed necessary. The third, fourth, and fifth chapters are critical studies of Clark's three novels; and the sixth is an analysis of his short novel, *The Watchful Gods*. The seventh chapter—which includes brief discussions of the poetry, selected short stories, and the essay-story entitled "The Writer and the Professor"—is designed to offer tentative conclusions about the accomplishment and relevance of Walter Clark. Included also are a chronological chart and an annotated bibliography.

I want to offer very special thanks to Miss Kathleen Blow

(reference librarian at the University of Texas at Austin) and Mr. Charles Dwyer (reference librarian now at Sam Houston State College) for much patience and kindness and for their incredible ability to find any information I wanted. Mody Boatright, Roger Abrahams, Americo Paredes, and Anthony Hilfer (colleagues at the University of Texas at Austin) have at one time or another offered useful criticisms and suggestions for additional reading. John R. Milton (University of South Dakota), Richard Etulain (Northwest Nazarene College), William J. Handy (University of Oregon), J. Golden Taylor (Colorado State University), Delbert Wylder (Bemidji State College), and Stanley Alexander (Stephan F. Austin College) have all offered much-needed help. Robert Bly, Frederick Manfred, and the late Alan Swallow have taken time from the more important task of their own writing to send encouragement and to offer stimulating suggestions. Walter Van Tilburg Clark and my wife, Frankie Lea, have shown a kindness and a helpfulness no critic or husband ever deserved.

MAX WESTBROOK

The University of Texas at Austin

Contents

Chronology

1909   Walter Van Tilburg Clark born August 3, East Orland, Maine; son of Walter Ernest and Euphemia Abrams Clark; the first of four children.

1917   Clark's father, the son of a Methodist minister, resigned as Head, Department of Economics, City College of New York; became President, University of Nevada, Reno, Nevada, serving in this capacity until 1937.

1917– Attended Orvis Ring Grammar School and Reno High
1926   School, graduating in 1926.

1926– Attended University of Nevada, earning B.A. and M.A. de-
1931   grees; associated with campus theater and magazines, played varsity tennis and basketball, wrote a creative master's thesis on Tristram legend, concentrated on English literature and on European and American philosophers.

1932   *Ten Women in Gale's House and Shorter Poems.*

1931– Teaching Assistant, University of Vermont, concentrating
1933   on American literature and Greek philosophers. Critical thesis on Robinson Jeffers (dated 1934). Married in Elmira, New York, October 14, 1933, to Barbara Morse. Began ten years of teaching and coaching basketball at Cazenovia, New York.

1938   *The Ox-Bow Incident* written.

1940   *The Ox-Bow Incident* published; contrary to widespread belief, novel not based on a particular incident; movie script not written by Clark.

1945   *The City of Trembling Leaves.* O. Henry First Award for "The Wind and the Snow of Winter."

1946   Lived in Taos, New Mexico.

1949   *The Track of the Cat.* Lived on a ranch in Washoe Valley, Nevada.

1950   *The Watchful Gods and Other Stories.* Lived in Virginia City, Nevada.

1953   Resigned from University of Nevada "to protest 'autocratic' administration of the institution." Rockefeller Foundation Lecturer in Creative Writing, during spring term, at Reed College, University of Oregon, and University of Washington.

1954   Assistant Professor of English, University of Montana, Missoula, Montana.

1955   Father died.

1956   Began five-year association with San Francisco State College, serving the last three years as Director of Creative Writing.

1957   Witness for the defense in *Howl* obscenity trial.

1958   Honorary Litt.D., Colgate University.

1960–   Fellow in English (creative writing) at Center for Ad-
1961   vanced Studies, Wesleyan University, Connecticut.

1961   Mother died. Clark's son, Robert Morse, graduated from Stanford University (his daughter, Barbara Anne, now Mrs. Ross Salmon).

1962   Returned to Reno, Nevada, as Writer in Residence, editing papers of Alfred Doten for University of Nevada Press, teaching creative writing.

1966   Joined at University of Nevada by his son, Robert, a Ph.D. candidate in English, now writing on his own.

Walter Van Tilburg Clark

CHAPTER 1

The Long and Ancient Memory: Early Years and Literary Credo

F OR religious man," writes Mircea Eliade, "space is not homogenous; he experiences interruptions, breaks in it; some parts of space are qualitatively different from others." Some parts of space, that is, are considered sacred, thought to have an identity under and a connection with the real. Other parts of space are found to be "not sacred and so are without structure or consistency, amorphous." [1] The significance Eliade wishes to emphasize is that "the religious experience of the nonhomogeneity of space is a primordial experience, homologizable to a founding of the world, [for] it is the break effected in space that allows the world to be constituted." [2]

One characteristic of the religious man, it follows, is that space —whether the mountain and lake of nature or the home and backyard of modernity—is real according to how well the sensibility of the religious man can use it for the discovery of primordial reality, that reality which is the original, the thing in itself, as distinguished from all our intellectual and institutional formulations *about* the real. Only the man-made or profane value of space can be determined according to its economic value, its contributions to social prestige.[3]

In this sense of the word, Walter Van Tilburg Clark is religious, a sacred man in the twentieth century. He meets Eliade's definition, specifically, in that he believes "nothing can begin, nothing can be *done*, without a previous orientation," [4] and that a sacred view of space is the only possible ground of orientation. He qualifies also because he believes that a profane attitude toward space leads only to confusion, to disorientation, to loss of identity and meaning. Witness, for example, the rational analysis of space by the profane Curt in *The Track of the Cat* and the dizzying

[23]

confusion that results. I do not mean to suggest that Clark is merely an addendum to the sacrality Eliade describes or that sacrality is Eliade's personal property. Clark's version of this ancient tradition is his own. He has—to use a term Clark has often used in talking about other writers—his own *difference*. If we read his works, however, or take him at his own word, we see that Clark's affinities are fundamentally with Eastern thought; and the sacrality of space as described by Eliade is an essential part of Clark's heritage. The effort to understand Clark as a man and as a writer can best begin, I think, with a study of his individual experiences with that heritage.

I   *The Artist as Student*

Clark was born August 3, 1909, in East Orland, Maine, the son of highly educated parents, a fact which is important in the life of a man who has become perhaps the best of Western writers. Clark's family heritage is not the ranch, the West, but a vital type of the academic. His father, Walter Ernest Clark, was Head of the Department of Economics in the City College of New York. A distinguished scholar and educator, he was awarded the French Legion of Honor for outstanding service in economics and education. In 1917 he moved his family to Reno, Nevada, where he was President of the University of Nevada from 1917 until 1937. This combination of the intellectual and the West is essential to an understanding of Walter Van Tilburg. To ignore either side, or the tension between the two, or to think of him as a "natural" Westerner who wrote *The Ox-Bow Incident* and was then made too critically conscious by academia (Davies' problem in *The Ox-Bow Incident* is relevant to Clark's own problem), or to call Clark an anti-intellectual is to oversimplify. He did grow up in the West, and nothing is more important to him than land and its meanings—a point to be developed later in this chapter—but his youth and his family were characterized as much by an atmosphere of sophisticated learning as by a love of nature.

Clark's mature interest in sacrality is thus an Americanized interest in the sense that the sacred is a value that is sought, that is needed as a purge of the corrupting intellect. It is a mistake, I think, to associate his heroes with the Noble Savage of James Fenimore Cooper, as some critics have done.[5] Clark's characteristic hero is not an innocent becoming corrupted by alien forces; he is a nervously intellectual American seeking—or barely holding onto—an eminent sacrality that is under constant attack both from the divisive forces of civilization and from his own temptations to accept a part of himself as his whole self. The intellectual —in life and in art—is for Clark a legitimate if noisome part of this wholeness.

The education of young Clark, furthermore, was quite varied, including for example a considerable training in the fine arts. The chief influence here was probably his mother, Euphemia Abrams Clark. A graduate of Cornell University, she did advanced study in piano and composition with the famous Edward MacDowell of Columbia University, and gave up a possible career in music only when she became more interested in settlement-house work at Greenwich House in New York City, and, doubtless, in her four children, Walter, the eldest, Euphemia (born 1911), David (1913), and Miriam (1915). The breadth of education is reflected also in Clark's studies and activities while a college student. After attending Orvis Ring Grammar School and Reno High School (1917–26), he attended the University of Nevada (1927–31), earning both the bachelor's and the master's degrees. While at the University, he participated in Mask and Dagger (the campus theater group), played freshman and varsity basketball and tennis, wrote some for campus magazines and for the year book, enjoyed dating and dancing, went on hikes frequently and was especially fond of camping out, played chess, swam a good deal, continued—primarily as a listener—his interest in music, and wrote verse "constantly." [6]

Clark's thesis for his master's degree in English and philosophy is of special interest, partly because its subject will surprise those who think of him along with "Owen Wister and all those people." The full title is "Sword Singer: The Tale of Tristram Retold— With an Introductory Essay Concerning Sources of the Tristram Legend." The essay, pages I to XLVII, is designed to give "a general and immediately comprehensible survey of the outstanding decisions concerning sources of the Tristram legend, high points of its subsequent development, and explanation of such marked changes as have been incorporated." [7] "The Sword Singer," Clark's original 136-page version of the legend, forms the second part of his thesis.

The essay, despite occasional youthful excesses, is intelligent
and at times quite impressive in its knowledge and argumenta-
tion. Its major relevance for students of Clark's mature fiction is
that it provides a valuable insight into his early literary credo.
His attack on those who make a fetish of Malory reveals a strong
resentment of "scholarly sanctification," that is, praise of a work
merely because it is "old enough not to be certainly understood
in all its veins." [8] Legend, Clark believed then and now, is for the
present, not for the past, or at least not for the past alone. What,
then, is the place of myth in the mature fiction? In my own
reading of Clark, I reached the tentative conclusion that Clark
was concerned with myth, that he was knowledgeable on the
subject, that he was concerned with the kind of meaning normally
thought to be the property of myth, but that he worked by means
of his own myth-making abilities and not by redaction of specific
myths. When I wrote Clark of my feelings on this score, he
responded in full:

> I'm not using any established mythical patterns—granting that
> there is human continuity, and that the little man inside never
> really dies in any of us, and that if I were to feel any real interest
> in formal psychology—which I don't—I'd find Jung's historical
> perspective and archetypal figures a good deal more interesting
> and trustworthy than anything in Freud—it seems to me, quite
> simply and self-evidently, that America has never developed a
> myth of any real consequence or relevance and that very little
> from the old worlds can be made to bear upon American realities
> with any real force or validity. The effort is usually conspicu-
> ously contrived and unconvincing. The American myth is still
> to become, if there's ever going to be one—or several, for they
> will have to be various. Such effort as I've spent in that direc-
> tion then—has been given to trying to find patterns of conse-
> quence in the American reality which seem to me to have some
> potential of mythical quality—to trying to find myth, you might
> say, or some promise and foreshadowing of it—not to trying to
> apply myth. [9]

In this statement lies one of the most fundamental and most
consistently held of all the tenets of Clark's literary credo. The
artist cannot create through conscious reflection on words or
theories, nor can a life of vitality and integrity be based on words
or theories. Clark, it should be emphasized, is not saying that the

artist must sit with pencil poised, waiting for inspiration. His rejection of established myths as a mode of apprehension is a rejection of the belief (found, for example, in Kant and Emerson) that the rational mind has a generative authority. Clark quite aptly describes his work as a search for "patterns" which "have some potential of mythical quality," but established myths from "the old worlds" can be applied to American experience only through the offices of the rational mind. "The intellectual formulation," Clark wrote early in his career, "is always a result, not a beginning." [10] In 1962, the mature Walter Clark held this same belief. Speaking through the personae of a writer's soul, he admits that the "primal outpouring . . . is often more than a little crude and formless." Yet, when "you begin to think about the language, instead of just letting it find itself while you live the experience, you're out of the creative act and into the critical, which is quite another thing." [11]

The creative process must be uncalculated; the imagination can tap the generative power of the primordial only if it is freed from the divisive and stilted work of the rational mind. The artist's eye must be on the experience itself, for the rational mind cannot apprehend the thing itself. It can only comment *about* the experience. The end product, the work of art, is not free, however, of intellectual obligations. What the artist has seen in experience must be given communicable form, a shape that can meet the legitimate standards of the conscious mind. In his correspondence, for example, Clark warned me away from asking him about the meanings of his fiction. He was very pleasant about it, not at all truculent; and his reasons were not based on a resentment of criticism or of the rational mind, but on a carefully made distinction that would please the best of the formalist critics: the meaning one hoped to get into his work (the author's intention) and the meaning actually in a work were not necessarily the same; and criticism—that is, good criticism—was a fair test, at least potentially, of whether or not the author had succeeded.

Clark's literary credo, then, is based on his belief in the capacity of the unconscious mind to discover and to give shape to objective knowledge about the human experience. Only the unconscious mind is generative, capable of insight into the primal realities of life. The rational mind is equally a part of the human being, but its proper role is to function empirically, after experience; and to use the rational mind as if it had creative energies is to distort both the observer and the observed. The same assignments are found in Clark's comments on revision as a part of the creative process:

> . . . as often as not you'll spend most of your time in the critical phase; revision, though as the very word says, it is envisioning again, is preponderantly a critical act, in which much of the attention is given, unavoidably, to language. But you will never catch the life—without which nothing else matters—in the critical state, and even when you revise, you must, in order to test the language, envision *again*, repeat the experience. There's no other possible way of telling the right word from the wrong.[12]

Clark, I would like to repeat, is not advocating a non-intellectual inspirationalism. Experience must be looked at through the unconscious mode, but the artist is responsible to a standard which exists objectively, apart from any man's conscious or unconscious experience. The artist's work is not legitimate merely because he felt it that way. There is a "right word" and there is a "wrong word," and the artist is obliged to *think* with his myth-making faculties and to think with discipline for the "right word" to result.

Clark's emphasis on the experience itself and his respect for critical principles appear with unapologetic clarity in the judgments he makes in his first master's thesis. According to Clark, Swinburne's Tristram "fights, loves, rows, and dies in rimed couplets admirably suited to meditations in a pansy garden. A great storm comes upon the boat at sea with all the terror and supernatural force of a splashing in the goldfish bowl. Tristram is a parlor poet and Isolt is a weak minded consumptive." [13] Swinburne is writing *about* the legend; he is not experiencing it. Clark does give Swinburne credit for changes leading to a "greater unity and more elevated emotional tone," [14] but Tennyson's version is considered scarcely worth mentioning. Clark's favorite, the "dean of contemporary American poets," is Edwin Arlington Robinson.

Robinson's version of the Tristram legend is admired for its "restrained and perfected blank verse" and for its "psychological exactitude." [15] The poem becomes "tragedy, great tragedy, poignantly real, powerfully gripping, and yet so conceived by the true poet of dramatic sense, that it never overstrains the bonds of masterful form, never slops over from tragedy into tragic melodrama." Form, then, is not merely external to art; it is intrinsic, inseparable, necessary. Clark goes even farther away from inspirationalism by saying that Robinson, in the final analysis, is a "poet of thought." It is in the "underlying conception that we must find the vitality he unquestionably has. Words, with him, are not ideas, but meticulously exact conductors to ideas. He has a queerly far-seeing ability to reproduce things as they are, as they must have been, making words what they should be—merely mediators between reality and reality recreated." [16]

In these early studies, Clark was developing principles which would later motivate the theme and structure of his best fiction. Consistently, he disparages the rational mind for its tyranny over feeling, for its insidious separation of man from his whole self and from his vital connection with the archetypes of human experience. The separation is destructive of man's natural response to life; it blurs his sight, dulls his feeling, dims his sense of sound. The damage caused by the villainy of the rational mind can be healed only by returning to the source, by getting back—without intellectual intercession—to concrete experience. Such are the grounds on which he condemns Swinburne's Tristram as a papier-mâché creature, built of words only.

Clark's position makes one think of what is, at least in a general way, an American tradition of the unchained artist: of Walt Whitman and his desire to "start with the sun," of Thomas Wolfe and his famous philippic against Fitzgerald's suggestion that creativity must be critical and selective as well as emotionally vital, or perhaps of the scholarly defense of this tradition in the work of Karl Shapiro, James Miller, Bernice Sloate, and others. The association, however, is misleading. Form, to Clark, is not the enemy of art, but a power of art. His desire is not to escape thought or to defy the just claims of the rational mind but to make thought felt, to give blood to ideas and bones to meaning, to discover form. Unlike Whitman and Wolfe, who felt that selectivity was niggardly and undemocratic, Clark has always felt that selectivity was essential to art.

Having studied philosophy with deep appreciation, Clark does not fall into the philosophical naïveté of those who use reason to condemn reason, who condemn form while trying to give form to their condemnation. Clark, on the contrary, places a high value on reason, on form, even on abstract thought. His point is that all three are a medusa for the artist engaged in the creative process: to look on them is to die. The only way to write or to live is through a ritualistic devotion to experience itself. This devotion makes Clark a religious man and explains the sacred role of land in his art. The conscious mind cannot use the medium of words to contact primordial reality. Only the unconscious mind can sense the real, and the unconscious does not work by will or by words. It works as an attitude, a religious sense, and its material is land, place. For the typical American, this concept does not make sense: man cannot think land. Clark, of course, would agree—if it is assumed that thinking is the exclusive property of reason. What he does believe is that the unconscious can discover the shape of a land, can hear and touch primordial reality itself as distinguished from the conscious mind's rational words *about* reality. Clark walks the world with respect, with ritualistic attention to the character of the land.

And ritual, be it remembered, is neither free nor arbitrary. It requires form in accord with standards that exist outside the individual. Reason and form, then, are real; but they must come after the fact of experience. The artist concentrates on the experience itself, letting it come into him with its own shapes and sounds and smells, letting experience work ("hatch" is the word Clark uses) within his unconscious self. Then, if the artist has done well, the form occurs, comes into being, and can meet the requirements of intelligent criticism. To start with form, idea, or reason is a profanation of man and his art. The desire to express in art that which can be seen only when the unconscious is allowed to contact the primal reality and the desire to make that expression viable for this time and this country have been the central ambitions of Clark's artistry.

II *Jeffers and Jung*

In 1931, Clark returned to the New England of his birth to accept a teaching assistantship at the University of Vermont, where he continued his graduate study of literature and philosophy. At the University of Nevada, he had concentrated on English literature and on European and American philosophers. At the University of Vermont, he concentrated on American literature and on Greek philosophers, poets, and dramatists. In 1934, he completed a thesis entitled "A Study in Robinson Jeffers" and received his second master's degree. Commenting on Jeffers' life, art, and ideas, Clark develops his essay by comparisons with Wordsworth, Swinburne, and the Greeks. It is quite possible that Jeffers exercised much less influence on Clark than is commonly supposed, for Clark came to Jeffers as one comes in an unexpected place to a sudden friend. There may have been more recognition than influence. Clark's early study of Jeffers, nevertheless, is important.

Clark met Jeffers at Thor House and was immediately impressed. He had already become a close reader and deep admirer of Jeffers' poetry; now he came to like the man, his famous Thor House, and his beloved and rugged California coast. It is clear from Clark's comments that he was attracted most profoundly by Jeffers' love of nature, his "contact with earth and air." [17] More significant, however, is the quickness and strength of Clark's attack on those who said that Jeffers' love of nature was animalistic or negativistic. People who read Jeffers as saying "it does not matter what happens to men" [18] are flatly wrong. They have, Clark contends, taken a part of a thought for a complete thought. They have failed to see Jeffers' insistence on the right of "the individual to his own best fulfillment independent of his fellows." [19] Clark's affinity for Jeffers is best explained in his description of the values he thinks one should see in Jeffers' poetry:

Jeffers postulates inherent force, call it what you please, God, Power, Will, Electricity, Entelechy. It is this scientific pantheism which, more than anything else, lends the repute of mysticism to much of his work. And truly, in any ultimate sense, there is little to distinguish between the informing force of science and the God-in-all of the pantheists. Only Jeffers must not be conceived as going beyond this conception of God to any belief in mystic unity of the individual with the central source, any unity, that is, beyond like physical basis. Death is death, with Jeffers, and the personality is disintegrated, though the physical components continue to exist. There is nothing more mystical in his belief than in any good electronic theory, which is mystery enough, goodness knows, but nothing in which the individual may lose his sense of being an individual, the true test of mystics.[20]

What Clark found in Jeffers' poetry is not, of course, what we are supposed to find in Clark's own writings; nor are we to assume that Clark did not grow and change after his early work as a master's degree candidate in college. The relevance of the early years, however, should not be overlooked. Two points are of special importance. First, Clark does not consider that there is, "in any ultimate sense," a significant difference between the force of science and the force of God. He is willing to "call it what you please, God, Power, Will, Electricity, Entelechy." To the American of a typical Judeo-Christian upbringing, this concept will come as a shocking admission of metaphysical irresponsibility. But to Clark—as to anyone who believes in Jungian archetypes —you may call "it" what you will because the conscious mind of the individual is not capable of assessing ultimate reality, because a commitment to the sacrality of place is a commitment to local gods, to many gods, to reality as it is sensed (not reasoned out) by the unconscious. It is, then, the conscious mind, man's arrogant intellect, which may call "it" what it will; for the verbal choices of the rational mind are more likely to blur than to designate the nature of the ultimate.

The second point of importance in the passage quoted above is Clark's understanding of unity and individualism. He admires a unity between man and his universe; but, as I hope to show in chapters on Clark's major fiction, he never thinks of unity as a state achieved or as a fixed accomplishment. He seems almost to undercut the effort itself with intellectual ironies, and he includes an implicit rejection (explicit in his non-fiction) of the Oriental belief that the individual ego should merge with and be lost in a mystical unity. Clark is defending Jeffers against an interpretation he thinks is mistaken, but he is also defending Jeffers against an interpretation that he considers tantamount to an accusation.

Readers lacking an affinity for Western sacrality will find Clark's position evasive. Since, in his four main volumes of fiction, he is concerned with unity, why does he reject the mystical unity of the East? How is it possible to seek unity with the all and yet cling to one's own ego? The answer, for all men who hold the conscious mind to be our primary mode of apprehending ultimate reality, is that it is not possible. What Clark means by unity does not make sense if we analyze his meanings according to the theme of unity associated with studies of William Blake, William Wordsworth, Ralph Waldo Emerson, or James Fenimore Cooper. In order to understand what unity does mean to Clark, in order to find his literary context, we must begin with that way of thinking which emphasizes the unconscious mind as a means of contacting archetypal patterns. The fundamental assumptions of that thinking may be represented by the following quotation from C. G. Jung: "Whether he understands them or not, man must remain conscious of the world of the archetypes, because in it he is still a part of Nature and is connected with his own roots. A view of the world or a social order that cuts him off from the primordial images of life not only is no culture at all but, in increasing degree, is a prison or a stable." [21]

For the man of sacrality, a formulated ontology is the work of the rational mind; and it is a work doomed to failure. Our only contact with primordial reality is through the archetypes, and the archetypes speak only to the unconscious. Thus Clark values unity, for he uses the word to describe man's contact with the primordial, but the unconscious mind lacks the ability to formalize its contacts into words and theories, and thus Clark, on the topic of ontological status, moves back in a way that seems evasive. From his own viewpoint, he is not retreating from his theory of unity; he is realistically admitting the inability of the unconscious mind to fully satisfy a modern ego, and he is avoiding the "prison" or "stable" that man builds for himself when he insists that the conscious mind must take the responsibility of theorizing about ultimate reality.

"The more independent 'reason' pretends to be," Jung writes, "the more it turns into sheer intellectuality which puts doctrine in the place of reality and shows us man not as he is but how it wants him to be." [22] In this statement, rather than in mysticism or pantheism or in Cooper, is one essential reference point of the context of Walter Clark. From early in his career, Clark believed that literature, like life, could not be the province of reason severed from some other way of knowing, some way that put man into more direct contact with the primordial. That other way was, more than anything, the experiencing of place, of the land in which one lived. It is this restraint of the rational mind before an archetypal sense of sacred space which attracted the young Clark to the poetry of Robinson Jeffers.

There are profound differences, of course, between Clark and Jeffers and between the Clark of the 1930's and of the 1940's. During his apprenticeship, for example, Clark was more attracted to thoughts of perfection than a later maturity would permit. As a master's degree candidate, Clark praised Jeffers' poem entitled "Fauna"; for he found in it a cycle "from the restless, idealized, inexperienced desire, through the trial of purely physical satisfaction, which is found lacking, into the final fulfillment which combines the ideal with the physical, and is resultantly blessed with perfection." [23] In his own early poems and stories, especially in his fables, Clark was at least beguiled by comparable cycles. An even greater difference is that at no point in his career has Clark despaired so fundamentally of man's moral efforts as has Jeffers. What Clark did find in Jeffers was a poetry that measured up to his own most consistent principles: first, man is "deeply influenced by the land he lives on" [24] and he can contact the primordial only through the language of land, place; and, second, the writer must evoke in the reader the reality itself, must convey the primordial reality in the only way it can be conveyed. If he evokes only the intellectual associations of that reality, he has failed.

Jeffers, as read by Clark in his apprentice years, measures up to these two principles. Jeffers' ability to create the emotion itself, Clark held, caused him to shock some readers. What the Greek dramatists and poets did for their age, but cannot do for ours, Jeffers was felt to have done for the twentieth century. His poetic emotions are real, not merely a harmless presentation about the emotion. "We are aware, in Jeffers," Clark writes, "of the living act: in the Greeks of an *expression* of the act." [25] This distinction, the most fundamental principle in Clark's literary credo, helps to explain his attraction to the mystic's refusal to program knowledge, his belief in the pantheist's recognition of man's kinship with nature, his belief that the intellect lacks generative capability, and his distrust of rituals which are borrowed from other cultures. Like Emerson, Clark would say that no one can experience for you: the touch of sacrality cannot be felt at secondhand. Unlike Emerson, Clark believes that experience will expose in nature a shocking variety of benign and ominous gods.

III *Teacher and Reader*

There is considerable evidence, however, to suggest that an American type of decency has been, in Clark's life as in his writing, a constant companion to his Orientalism. Alan Swallow and Wallace Stegner have made a similar observation about Western writers generally,[26] and Clark's devotion to his duties as a teacher of creative writing is additional testimony. The loyalty of a legion of friends is further evidence. The facts of his adult life, certainly, like those of his schoolboy days, reveal a certain restlessness, perhaps even some signs of insecurity, but nothing exotic.

On October 14, 1933, in Elmira, New York, he married Barbara Morse, who was to bear him two children, Barbara Anne, now Mrs. Ross Salmon and the mother of three children of her own, and Robert Morse, who was graduated from Stanford in 1961 and has since served as an intelligence officer in the United States Air Force. After ten years as a teacher and coach in Cazenovia, New York, interrupted in 1940 with a year at Indian Springs in southern Nevada, Clark moved West to stay. Except for brief visits to Mexico and Canada, he has never traveled outside the United States. He spent 1946 in Taos, New Mexico; lived four years on a ranch in Washoe Valley, Nevada; spent five years in Virginia City, Nevada; was Head of Creative Writing for three years at the University of Montana; and taught five years at San Francisco State College, spending the last three as Head of the Creative Writing Section. In between, he has taught regular sessions at the University of Nevada, Stanford, and the University of Iowa Writers Workshop—not to mention his attendance at numerous conferences in creative writing and his frequent appearances on television and radio in programs devoted to writing. Recently, he has been back in Reno, Nevada—which is more than any other place his home town—working on the papers of Alfred Doten, Western chronicles held by the University of Nevada.

This rather extensive experience is not ancillary to Clark's art. He has been from the first acutely conscious of the craft of writing, perhaps too conscious; and his sincere devotion to helping others interested in acquiring that craft has occupied an inordinate amount of his time and energy. His habit of staying for an extended period of time in a given locale in the West and the fact that he has not yet been to Europe are also indicative of this man's character. Even in his reading habits we find evidence of an open-mindedness which does not fit any stereotype. His favorite writers, he says, are "too many to name, and too various to indicate anything." [27] Writers of whom he has "made pretty thorough examination" he lists in the following manner: "Homer, Aeschylus, Laotse, Chuang Tsu, Jeffers, Wallace Stevens, Kafka, Melville, [Henry] James, Dostoievski, Chekov, Crane, both Hart and Stephen, T. S. Eliot, Conrad, Hardy, Hemingway, Faulkner, Willa Cather, W. H. Hudson, Thomas Mann, D. H. Lawrence, Turgenev, Katherine Ann Porter, Eudora Welty, John Steinbeck, Eugene O'Neill, G.B.S., Mark Twain, Whitman, Thoreau." Clark describes this list, furthermore, as merely illustrative, not complete.

In returning to favorites, he tends to select a poem, play, or novel rather than an author. The illustrative list, again, is catholic: "*The Ambassadors, Crime and Punishment, Green Mansions, Moby Dick* and *The Confidence Man, Heart of Darkness* and *Nostromo, Death Comes for the Archbishop, The Bear* and *Light in August, Sons and Lovers* and *The Man Who Died, Buddenbrooks* and *Death in Venice, Walden, Macbeth,* 'Song of Myself.' " In addition, he reads a good deal, though irregularly, in history, preferring personal accounts, journals (*The Oregon Trail* and the journals of Lewis and Clark and of John Fremont are listed as examples); and he likes to read around in books on "astronomy, geology, bugs, beasts, fishes, dinosaurs, trees—all kinds—and weather."

That Clark has no particular political allegiance but registers as a Democrat to vote in primaries would probably surprise no one. His readers could probably guess also that he has no denominational faith. And his strong preference for "oriental faiths and philosophies" over the faiths and philosophies of European cultures would surprise only those who think of Clark as a writer of superior cowboy novels. Specifically, he lists as preferences "Hinduism, Buddhism, Confucianism, Taoism and all primitive faiths, philosophies, folklores, especially those of the American Indians," because they strike him as "unifying and inclusive," whereas the beliefs of occidental philosophers he finds to be "divisive."

What then is Clark's personal unity? What sense does it make to be vitally interested in basketball and academic freedom,[28] in Buddhism and cowboys, in C. G. Jung and Henry James? What realistic relation is there between tennis and the American dream or between a master's thesis on Robinson Jeffers and the practical needs of the American economy and culture? The answer, though disturbing to anyone with a passion for obvious action, is eminently practical; and it can be stated quite simply. Clark has believed, from his college days to the present, that it is realistic to seek contact with primordial values, that it is unrealistic to deny the power of archetypal energies and meanings in all men, and that the only way to contact the primordial honestly is to do it in contemporary terms.

He is concerned with various sports and with academic knowledge quite simply because sports and academic life are important in his own life and in the lives of millions of Americans. He is concerned with Hinduism and with ranch life because both may become exercises in sacrality. Thus the place of land in his own life and in his art, for land is the stuff of one's existence, the place one occupies, the personal context that must be observed with respect if knowledge is to be real rather than a collection of somebody else's words *about* reality. To deny the presence of tennis and the importance of economics in our lives is to fall into escapism, perhaps into a nostalgic desire to return to some past time. To deny the sacrality of America today is to sell out to the shortsighted practicalist and to the man of "reason" who would restrict reality to that which man's ego can encompass—that is, to nothing outside our *selves*. Clark's literary efforts, then, are quests in search of the long and ancient memory, efforts to restore the capacity of the unconscious to hear the archetypal voices of primordial reality; but they are efforts to do this in contemporary terms, in terms that may lead to real knowledge of the present rather than to indoctrination about the past.

Admittedly, Clark has struck a snag; but his quest for sacrality in an age of science and materialism is admirable in a way critics have not yet realized. And it is more than that: Clark has refused to ignore either the curse of history or the excitement that comes when we touch the real. What price he has paid for that refusal is known only to himself; but, for men who live between the Protestant Ethic and 1984, the price must seem a bargain. It is certainly worth investigation.

CHAPTER *2*

The Western Esthetic

WHEN the artist in the West begins the study of his legacy, he finds it is at once the most concrete and the most abstract of any regional legacy in America. He finds himself committed to the land, to an intimate knowledge of nature; and his commitment is specific, detailed. He is obliged to know the color of the hawk's wings, the name of the small cold lake farther up the mountain, and how to catch the trout which swim there. Without such experience and knowledge, he is a tourist, a dude. He is bookish and in disgrace. Along with an inherited duty to know and to respect the land comes the onus of the American dream—and with an insidious twist. The West, in the vision of so many of its artists, has the obligation to restore, or at least to husband, the American dream *after* it has already been corrupted in the East, the South, and the Midwest. Frederick Jackson Turner's famous thesis on the frontier, in fact, may be more applicable to Western literature than to Western history. Certainly, a substantial number of Western writers believe that Western experience (Westering, a way of life, whatever one's geographical fortunes may be) is the nation's best chance of healing the wounds caused by the Puritans when they made us feel ashamed of our bodies, afraid of the voice that comes from our dark and inner selves, apologetic for our worldly ambitions. Western writers have thus faced anew the ancient and sometimes American hope—the effort to discover the unity of body, soul, and land.

Between values and action, however, there is need for the stuff of continuing history. The nostalgic regionalist and the minor local colorist aside, a regionalist seeks that excitement which comes from realizing that what his countrymen have done is not yet known and will never be fully known so long as the study of the past continues to shock with new revelations about the meaning of today and to inspire fresh hopes and untold fears for the future. For the New England regionalist, Puritanism is but one of the forces of a continuing history which stretches from the landing of the *Mayflower* to the present, or at least to World War II. The meanings of Southern history—whether praised, damned, or evaluated judiciously—are intrinsic to the most contemporary Southern imagination.

I   *The Loss of Historical Continuity*

The Western imagination, by contrast, is denied a historical continuity. The artist looks to a heritage which has neither continued nor declined. It has stopped. He is caught, as it were, with his abstractions in his hand. He finds it difficult to write fiction in which the meanings of the past are brought to bear on contemporary problems. The history of the American Indian in the West may seem a rich source for cultural and literary purposes, but contemporary economics and politics in the West are not shaped by that history so much as by the energies of a Westering Babbitt who came from a bordering culture. The cowboy experience, in which profound ethical problems were realistically related to the economy of a burgeoning society, once spread its influence over a large area. But the cattle drives lasted only a brief time—a quarter of a century at most—and they ended abruptly. It was much the same with trapping, buffalo hunting, and gunfighting. Even the frontier farmer has not been found to exercise a relevance in the contemporary Western civilization he helped make possible, at least not in the way that antebellum slave holders are relevant to the contemporary South or seventeenth-century Puritans to twentieth-century New England. The Western artist—wanting to avoid the various forms of disunity he associates with Eastern and Southern decadence, hoping to exploit in living and in writing the lessons in unity he feels in the vastness and the weight of nature in the West—is covetous of action. Yet the kind of action he values seems to have taken place in the past, seems available today only in weekend sports, in a summer and suspect ranch, in sublimated forms that lack connection with socio-economic realities.

The problem of historical continuity gives rise to another problem, one which does not lend itself to neat explanations. The artist in the West finds himself in a strained relation with his national heritage. He is aware of the obvious economic and cultural importance of the West to the nation as a whole, and there is ample evidence also of his realization that the Western writer's search for continuity is not unlike the early New Englander's search for a history which—at least until the Civil War —had not yet been running long enough to *be* a history. Furthermore, all serious Western artists that I have read reveal their interest in the national—indeed, the universal—implications of their insight into regional experience.

The larger affinities of the Western writer, however, are subject to frustrations. The centers of literature and learning have long been in the East; and, although the South and the Midwest have won some respectability, a serious artist in the West may find himself, at any moment, slandered by Eastern and uninformed generalizations. Serious Western writers, it is true, are accustomed to having their best works blurred with the films of Roy Rogers. One can make a family joke of that kind of thing. Surely, it will pass, one can say. But beneath the lack of understanding lies a fundamental difference between the Western artist and the national culture of which he considers himself an alien member.[1]

That difference can be stated. Varying segments of the American culture recognize a meaning which cannot be assessed by the rational faculty. This non-rational meaning may be associated with religion, with the human spirit, with insight or sensitivity, with nature or the soul, or with what we may call "intuitive knowledge." In the East, the Midwest, and the South, intuitive knowledge is, most characteristically, a property of the conscious mind. In the Western esthetic, intuitive knowledge is a property of the unconscious mind. An intuition in the service of the conscious mind may have primarily an ethical function and thus acquire the prestige of philosophy without the formulations of philosophy. Hemingway's heroes, for example—most clearly his early heroes—are capable of moral insight apart from the offices of a rationale. Jake Barnes' efforts in brotherhood in *The Sun Also Rises* are dependent on his intuitive ability to sense the needs of his fellow man, and his efforts are meant to represent genuine ethical values. Yet Jake's metaphysics consists of little more than a vaguely serious wish that he could be a better Catholic. Frederic Henry in *A Farewell to Arms* is sensitive to the feelings of the Priest; and it is manifest that his sensitivity is a virtue, a genuine virtue, not an illusion. Yet his comments on ultimate reality, both before and during Catherine's dying, are unremittingly negativistic. A firm stance on metaphysics, in fact, is usually associated with insensitivity and, therefore, with villainy. Hemingway's early heroes are forced to make-do with a code, with ethical values discovered by the individual's insight and lacking the sanction of metaphysical formulation.

II *Two Types of Intuition*

Characteristic Western heroes may or may not have the Hemingway type of sensitivity; but, in either case, their intuition is grounded in the unconscious mind and carries metaphysical implications. The two types of intuition are not always and rigidly separated, but the distinguishing Western viewpoint is that to make intuition the property of the conscious mind is to assign to reason the impossible task of contacting ultimate reality. Since metaphysics is primary to ethics, since it is the intuition and not the reason which can contact the real, the man of conscious intuition is thought to have taken the only means of getting beyond reason and to have confined it to the service of reason.

Conscious intuition is obviously a non-rational mode of apprehension, but the insights it produces are within the compass of the rational mind. While it would be impossible, for example, to make a rational explanation of the bullfight substitute for the ability to see and to feel its meanings, as Jake Barnes cannot with words make Robert Cohn see and feel, it is nonetheless true that a rational explanation of the values of the bullfight is sufficiently clear to the reason. The insights of unconscious intuition, by contrast, are offensive to reason when rendered into words. The man of reason is free to dislike Jake Barnes' intuitive appreciation of bullfighting, but his values require him to approve of Jake Barnes' distinction between the good will of Romero and the corrupt will of bullfighters who seek praise for a courage they do not have. In Walter Van Tilburg Clark's *The City of Trembling Leaves,* however, Tim Hazard's intuition can be formulated only in terms of friendly and unfriendly gods; and the formulation contradicts reason's requirement that knowledge be consistent and coherent according to rational standards.

The artist in the West faces, therefore, difficult problems from within and from without, problems which push him to bold and —sometimes—strained efforts. He feels an obligation to be, as it were, both Whitman and Dreiser at one and the same time. He believes in the sacred unity that can be apprehended only by the unconscious intuition, and he recognizes the lot of the democratic American, the man committed to a conscious and self-conscious struggle on behalf of the individual in a land that is holy and yet profane, potentially sacred yet suffering from massive exploitation. Differing versions of the Western esthetic—from the most successful to the most stereotyped—can best be understood, I think, in terms of their varying methods of handling or evading this difficult problem.

Central to the approach of the more successful Western writers is a belief in "primary realism," a term Clark has used to describe the recurrent human experience C. G. Jung calls "archetypal." [2] This realism is deeper than that of the "narrow factualist" whose refusal to accept the archetypal forces and wonders of life causes him to define man as merely a product of environment, despite the fact that a "product" does not develop an ulcerous guilt, or go trembling into puberty, or feel the mystery of woman, or the awesomeness of God, or the necessity of a Christ, or the terror and beauty of death. Rejecting such spiritual cowardice, Clark holds that man's beliefs must accommodate both the brute force of nature and the affirmation of nature. A realist supposedly bases his belief on what is, but the *is* of the universe includes the brutality and indifference which so impressed the naturalist, as well as the empathy and meaning which so impressed the romanticist.

"Primary realism," based on archetypal realities which are deeper than either the facts or the theories of modern man, is thus inclusive without being eclectic. It is man's intellect which presumes to separate dream from fact, which insists that man must pay allegiance to one or the other. It is man's insistence on rational understanding which drives him into the dark corners of existentialism, where he must leap, apologetically, into a pretension his reason cannot fuel into faith, or else do without God, do without the sense of any meaning to human existence. [3] Intuition must serve the unconscious mind, Clark believes, because it is the intuition—and not reason—which has the toughness to sense the infinite variety of man and his universe. To put intuition in the service of reason is to imprison it in an intellect which demands consistency on its own terms. To seek a unity which betrays the variety of man and his universe is to run the supreme risk, is to be fatally unrealistic.

III   *"Primary Realism" and the Critics*

Clark's "primary realism" and the broad tradition of Western sacrality, of which it is a part, have not won favor in prestigious literary circles; the praise that has been won is usually tainted with apology, with attempts to justify a given work as good history or good craftsmanship and thus of merit despite its being Western.[4] The most notorious voices of Western criticism, unfortunately, have not done much to help the general understanding of the literature whose cause they support. One well-known but partisan critical study of the tradition of sacrality is *Start With the Sun* by Karl Shapiro, James Miller, and Bernice Sloate. The book condemns the Puritans for separating man into flesh and spirit, praises Whitman for celebrating the wholeness of man and for exhorting Americans to return to the primal and generative source of life, and accuses T. S. Eliot of disrupting Whitman's healthy direction and returning American literature back into the old sickness of Puritan separativeness. But this accusation judges Eliot according to the standards of a tradition quite different from the one to which he gave allegiance, an embarrassing error for critics busily protesting the tendency to judge the Whitmanian tradition according to the standards of Eliot and the "New Criticism." More importantly, this is to ignore the fact that the *donnée* in American history is an extreme self-consciousness forced upon us by our constitutional claim that we would prove to the world the worth of individual man; and, further, no defender of sacrality should fault Eliot for facing honestly the barrenness of American individualism and the isolation that resulted or for his working out a resolution which can accurately be called a rediscovery of the establishment sacrality of high church and cultural traditions.

Even less helpful is the venture into criticism by an artist whose fiction is a major part of modern sacrality: D. H. Lawrence's *Studies in Classic American Literature*. Lawrence's adherence to the sacred tradition is unmistakable, and his pronouncements often carry force. He repeatedly emphasizes his belief that the unconscious is primary to the conscious, and he holds that to believe only what the intellect can grasp is to deny forces and meanings that cannot be denied. Yet he shows no understanding of American individualism, and he argues so dogmatically for the unconscious that he falls into the very divisiveness he is attacking. Lawrence, an extremist, chides Melville for an interest in reform of naval injustices. There is certainly a good deal of the perverse in Lawrence, a childish desire to shock the establishment out of its Babbittry; but *Studies in Classic American Literature* does little to help our understanding of the place of ethics in sacrality or of sacrality as a literary tradition.[5]

Closer to Clark's vision and closer to the center, I think, is John Steinbeck's theory of "non-teleological" thinking.[6] Steinbeck shows more sympathy for the American born into self-consciousness, and he is fully aware of the capacity of man to corrupt any tradition into tyranny. Basically, Steinbeck argues that ethical principles are primarily the product of reason and culture. As such they are not teleological. This does not mean that man should be non-ethical or unethical, but that there is a deeper reality to life, that man's reasoning about ethics is not a way to get at primordial reality. Man's reason turns him back upon himself, takes him away from teleology. There is, Steinbeck believes, another way to think.

This other way of thinking—a belief in the possibility of knowing through the unity of thought and things—is more than anything else the common denominator among the differing versions of sacrality. Real knowledge is said to be knowledge in things, not in words *about* things. Those who think only with their intellect —or with the emotional refractions of intellect frustrated—can believe in a benevolent God, an indifferent force, or in no God. The intellect simply cannot encompass all three. Yet man has the capacity, through the offices of the "little man inside" (the voice of intuition in the service of the unconscious), to sense God and no-God, to see in the things of life an unreasonable variety—if only he will admit that heresy into the court of his own intellect.[7]

IV *Five Basic Beliefs*

At least five characteristic beliefs follow from this central principle of the unity of thought and things. First, there is no answer of the type demanded by the intellect. For the sacred man of the American West, it is presumptuous to think an individual's intellect can formulate the infinite. Second, the end hoped for is not a state achieved but an attitude—felt but never owned—toward a reality which touches but which is never confined by the intellect. Third, what is commonly called evil is an intellectual confusion of forces which are an intrinsic part of man and nature; and it cannot be exorcised by the pathological flagellations of the intellect. These forces—brute drives, if you will, but not evil—can be appeased, shaped away from destructive action, only through the individual's courage to be human, to listen to those archetypal meanings which are given voice through the unconscious. Fourth, the Christian God is a concoction of the rational mind, an illusion of man's desire to have a comforting and personal attention from on high; for only the intellect could propose a God so out of keeping with human nature as the Christian God. God, to the sacred imagination, is plural, various. He includes both the non-rational cruelty of the Old Testament God and the love of the New Testament God. Man's intellect cannot conceive His face, but man's unconscious can sense His generative, primordial force. Fifth, the hope of man is to establish contact with the original, the source, to "start with the sun."

Clark's own version of these characteristic beliefs is distinguished in part by his awareness of the total American experience. The Clark hero is American, specifically, in that his heritage includes the Puritan scar. He too has been rent asunder, at least damaged or endangered, by the inheritance of a noisome consciousness—which may explain Clark's interest in and sympathy with the self-tortured and overly-analytical heroes of Henry James.[8] The need—and it is shared by Clark's ineffectual saints —is to heal the wound, to make of one's self a whole man restored from an inherited disjointment of body and spirit, an inherited separativeness from nature. It is in this sense, and in this sense only, that Clark's affinity for the nonintellectual can be understood. His heroes feel the weight of the American experience from Puritanism toward the American dream and into the barrenness of the individual ego. Not even the boy hero is free, pure, natural; even he is analytical, and consciously so.

It is fitting, therefore, that Clark's heroes do not deny the intellectual responsibilities of the ego they are born with and do not wish to banish. And it is fitting that one of Clark's favorite words is "balance," a sign of the precarious and yet historically realistic type of unity in which he believes. If the Clark hero can accept the burden of ego and yet hold the arrogant ambitions of the intellect in check, then perhaps he can touch primordial realities beyond the intellect, perhaps he can learn to walk quietly on this earth, attentive and respectful. Perhaps he can exorcise the evil of man's separation from nature and heal the psychic wounds of our modish severance of body from soul. If he can realize the balance that is in things, then unity will occur; and *occur* is the precise word. The rational faculty, of course, is offended by this word: if man respects a claim to ultimate reality without understanding the process of the claim, how is he to distinguish the genuine from the bogus? But here again, advocates of sacrality reply, is the arrogant intellect, insisting that it must know the workings of the primordial, betraying man's unconscious ability to distinguish between the authoritative voice of the primordial and the whims of personal bias. The rational mind can neither trace nor understand the workings of ultimate reality, but the unconscious can sense its authority.

The significance of the word *occur* in Clark's world view can scarcely be overestimated. When Clark added the ego to his concept of sacrality, he brought in also the will, a sense of individual responsibility that is different in kind from the role of the will in Oriental or primitivist sacrality; and the will is necessarily a function of the conscious mind. Clark grants, furthermore, the legitimate place of the will in the balance that he seeks; but he believes in the necessity of a partnership of faith between unconscious intuition and the reason. How the conscious reason and the unconscious intuition can form a partnership is, obviously, beyond the understanding of our rational minds. Thus a state of unity is a value which occurs. It may be sought, both by the advisory voice of the conscious mind and by the substantive voice of the unconscious intuition; but it cannot be programmed. It is an exercise in dedication, with full attention to the demands of the workaday world, and the disciple need not know its mystery. To ask for more is to ask that the real submit itself to the intellect's ability to name the real, is to limit nature to man instead of opening man to nature. Thus Clark finds a kind of answer in the process of questioning. Answers tend to close the matter and they invite smugness, but the man who questions may keep his mind open and his intuition alert.

The discipline of man's unconscious intuition is the topic of Chapter 6, but the role of faith in sacrality must be mentioned here. From the viewpoint of Western writers like Clark and Steinbeck, the Christian intellect has vitiated faith. The modern emphasis on reason (that which is within the area of human understanding) has left no meaningful place for faith (that which is beyond human understanding). Faith has come to be for the modern Christian not a vital mode of touching God but a cover-up for reason's inability to go all the way to God. When reason runs out, the Christian hides behind claims of faith; but he turns to cries of "faith" only as a last resort, only when his more admired reason has run into a chasm it cannot cross. Thus the modern Christian, according to practitioners of Western sacrality, is hard put to answer the child's question: why have faith in the Christian God rather than in any other God? And it is difficult to show the child how belief in the Christian God is any more than a cultural preference.

Faith, in the sacred tradition, must have ontological rather than merely cultural status. For sacred man, faith obtains to ontological status quite simply because the primordial speaks to the unconscious intuition with authority, with primordial authority.[9] The man of reason finds it difficult to hold such a position, for he has given a primary role to the individual ego; and if faith comes in the authoritative voice of God, how can the goodness of the individual be required? What virtue is there for a democratic individual in obeying the voice of absolute authority? The answer, according to the man of sacrality, is that man's individual virtue is a necessary condition of his hearing the voice. For the man of reason, faith is a dishonored prop to the limitations of reason; and the burden of ontological validation rests, impossibly, on man's rational capabilities. For sacred man, the validation rests in the only place possible—in the primordial source

—and man's role in the act of faith is to have the goodness and courage to hear and to heed.

None of this should suggest that religion for the sacred man is an easy thing. Clark is typical of Western artists at their best in his emphasis on balance; and balance—if it is to be realistic —is maintained in tension. To lose that tension is to lose all. On one side, the Clark hero finds the primitive, the innocent, the animal—that which enjoys the most unaffected contact with nature. On the other, he finds the intellectual and the materialist, those who have lost the capacity for generative action. The hero's quest is not a search for compromise, not a reasoned balance between the spiritual and the practical; rather, the quest is for a unity of thought and things, a dedication to learning how to think through the language of both the things of nature and the things of man.

V   *The Ancient World and the Modern Intruder*

But the hero's land—as nature or as civilization—has not been given to him in primitive innocence. The land has come into the hero's touch already tainted by history, as the hero himself is tainted by history. The American West is not—in the vision of its major contemporary artists—a land one grows up in. It is a land one goes to. The land, after all, belonged to the Indian before the white man came to exploit the West. For the white hero to appropriate Indian (or primitivist) traditions as a means of belonging to the land would be for him to take a conscious and therefore an intellectual and doomed approach to sacrality. Since Indian traditions are not intrinsic to the white man's own history, the appropriation would be calculated more than felt.[10] The Indian does in many stories teach the white hero, and he is certainly more worthy than men satiated by societal values; but primitive cultures cannot provide a unity with land for those Western writers who accept the mind as well as the body, the curse as well as the accomplishment of civilization.

Clark's hero, for example, even when born and raised on the land, is an initiate, a man on the edges. He is the intruder into someone else's nature, the outsider come into the domain of offended gods; and some of his judges watch his entrance with

love, some with malevolence. No associations can be fixed. The
soul is not just the center of goodness—limp, white, defenseless,
and pure—but seems to house also some most unholy energies.
Reason is only relevant at times, and it lacks the ability to pick
those times. God is not necessarily good or evil or even attentive.
In the soul, in reason, God, land: in all areas the hero finds good,
evil, and irrelevance.

The intellect cannot maneuver through such irrational possibilities. Only the unconscious intuition—the raucous and disturbing
homunculus of man's inner self—can face such perverse realities
and such multiplicity without panic. Still, man does have ethical
obligations to his profane and divisive history, to his time and
his place, else his allegiance is without language, is abstract. The
Western esthetic thus includes a characteristic belief in an ethical
obligation which has no intellectually recognizable connection
with the real. The ethical is typically associated with linear history and with the intellect, perhaps with a folk-sense of fair play
and with local ground rules; the real is associated with the dark
and primal self of man's inner being. A formulated connection
between the two would have to be a rational one, and the rational mind cannot cross from profane history into the cycles of
primordial reality except as empirical observer.

For most Americans and for modern man generally, this is
heretical. In European and American civilizations it has been
customary to ground ethics in reason, or to blur the traditional
distinctions of philosophy and to locate the ethical in church-
born habits or, even more loosely, in cultural stock-responses.
When grounded in folk terms, ethical principles are normally
granted metaphysical prestige without metaphysical responsibility. Since modern man is reluctant to advocate an ethic he cannot understand with his reason, and since man's reason cannot
create beyond itself, modern man has made for himself an ethical
code that lacks authority. And the incestuous process of man's
reason continues, doubling back on itself: the assignment of metaphysical prestige to an ethic of reason has caused modern man
to create a god who is merely a man of superior reason. But
when this superior man-god is given the responsibilities of the
real God and asked to provide and to constitute a rationale for
the neighborhood's code of fair play, the illusion is shown to be
so feeble that sophomoric questions are adequate to place the

man-god in metaphysical jeopardy: if man should be ethical (love his neighbor), why should not God also be ethical, why should He in His omnipotence create horrors for innocents? It follows for the man of reason that if there is no God, man must then find some other rationale for ethical belief; but the average man is not tough enough in his mind to go all the way with philosophy and not bold enough in his soul to accept the shock of sacrality. Modern man, therefore, is left dangling with his man-god and his doubts.

In their own individual ways, Clark and at least a dozen other successful Western American novelists have answered that the questions themselves are wrong. The essential connections of man and his universe are not subject to the verbal abstractions of the intellect. If we insist on confining knowledge to rational knowledge, then we can know nothing beyond our own powers to create; and man has created neither himself nor his universe, neither his reason nor his "little man inside." Western artists do not propose a formula—they would not be worth study if they did—but they do offer a direction, a possibility. If we reason about our place in linear time and learn to intuit with the unconscious our more fundamental place in primordial time, we have the possibility of maintaining an individual ego while feeling the generative power of our archetypal selves.

VI *The View From the Unconscious*

It is not appropriate, I assume, to conclude this chapter with a necessarily truncated presentation of the obvious qualifications. Andy Adams and Charles Siringo, typical of the authentic cowboy narrative, and Owen Wister and Eugene Manlove Rhodes, representative of romantic Western fiction, are clearly different from Walter Clark, John Steinbeck, Frederick Manfred, Vardis Fisher, Frank Waters, and several others I take to represent—not a dogmatic school—but an intrinsic tradition of Western literature. To do justice to variant versions of this tradition—Willa Cather's *O Pioneers!*, which is a curious use of sacrality as a better means to fulfillment of the Protestant ethic, or Wright Morris's *The Field of Vision,* which is a fascinating use of sacrality as a means of explaining how we have come to be in a wasteland—would require a scope far beyond that of the present study. It is appropriate, I think, to conclude with some tentative suggestions.

At least three conclusions seem justified. First, the emphasis on thought and things as a way of knowing has caused many Western artists to write each book as if it were a unique project. When the "things" change, so must the thought, the tone, the atmosphere. The author's voice behind the work may seem different in each work by that author. Critics who speak for a profane culture—with a firm belief in getting somewhere, amounting to something—want their art to reflect an economic psychology; and thus they are inclined to feel that an artist who does not start from youthful rebellion and move toward the resolution of old age is groping, has not found or fulfilled himself. Clark's three novels, for example, seem on first reading to have been written by three different novelists or by a single novelist who cannot resolve his artist's vision. Clark, however, is not attempting to move from one point in linear time to a culminating point in linear time. Steinbeck's capacity for treating each work as a separate entity has caused him to search for the sentimentality or idealism or harsh realism which he finds in the "things" of a given work; he does not view character and event from a predetermined metaphysics within the compass of the conscious mind. The primordial reality he seeks is deeper and more flexible. This has hurt his reputation with Eastern critics more attuned to the kind of continuity and consistency—found in Hemingway, for example—that is prompted by a devotion to linear time.

Second, the belief in unconscious intuition causes a basic shift from the norm in the relation of a hero (or of a character who is right in a given instance) to his author. The fallacy of message hunting granted, it is still more legitimate to associate the values of Hemingway with the values of his hero, or the values of Sinclair Lewis with the obvious implications of his social satire than it is to associate the values of Clark with those of Arthur Bridges in *The Track of the Cat* or the values of Steinbeck with those of Danny in *Tortilla Flat*. The reason is that writers who ground their art in conscious intuition must strike a more intimate relation between this intuition and ultimate reality than writers who feel that the conscious intuition is primarily social. Western writers do create heroes whose values are close to their own, but if you believe that reality is primordial then you believe that reality is less the property of any man's vision—including your own; you feel a certain generosity about man's theories, a generosity that would be a moral irresponsibility in a man who binds his ontology to the free will and responsibility of the individual's conscious ego.

Third, a writer who believes in sacrality takes an appoach to actuality which is disturbing and confusing to the expectations of readers accustomed to the art of a profane world view. The sacred man holds that it is necessary to ground one's self in the discipline of actual events, as does the writer of a profane tradition. But actuality to a sacred man is more real than expected in that it can manifest the primordial—tangibly—and yet less real than expected in that actual events are but the ephemera of the day, are not required to have a fidelity to conscious intuition sufficient to constitute a possible mode of apprehending ultimate reality. Belief in the integrity of natural objects is a necessary condition for belief in the free will and in the responsibility of the individual's conscious mind; and this view holds at least from Emerson to Hemingway. In the sacred world view, however, the voice of homunculus may speak a lie—in terms of reason's standards—which is the closest thing we know to the real and primordial truth.

Since Western writers are committed to their own time and yet believe in sacrality, the burden of the reader is to heighten his sensibility, to prepare himself for reading both the ritual swim of *The City of Trembling Leaves* and the shocking realism of the hanging in *The Ox-Bow Incident*. Both a capacity for naked purity and a capacity for brute murder are within each one of us, the Western artist believes. If we are to read him well, we must use our reason; but each reader must bring with him also his own homunculus.

CHAPTER 3

The Archetypal Ethic of
The Ox-Bow Incident

ONE of the most sensible of all critical principles warns the reader that he must not choose indiscriminately what questions he will ask of a work of art. To ask a significant question is to impose the conditions of possible meanings. Philosophers and literary theorists—Susanne Langer, for example, in *Philosophy in a New Key*—have written learned and convincing studies of the principle and its applications. The legal mind is alert to this principle in the courtroom, realizing that what is admitted as evidence depends as much on questions asked as on answers given. The practical critics of Walter Van Tilburg Clark's *The Ox-Bow Incident*, however, have allowed circumstances to mislead them into asking the wrong questions; and the evidence thereby granted relevance has led to confusion.

In 1940, when it was first published, *The Ox-Bow Incident* was immediately recognized as an exception, as a cowboy story of literary merit; and it is still conceded to be, on critical grounds, the best or at least one of the best cowboy novels ever written. Some such judgment has prompted reviewers and critics to ask why this cowboy story is superior to other cowboy stories. But the question suggests that the excellence of *The Ox-Bow Incident* consists in Clark's having handled skillfully what is normally not handled skillfully in works of sub-literary merit. The comparative approach might have worked if critics had used the fiction of Western writers like Willa Cather, John Steinbeck, Frederick Manfred, and Vardis Fisher. The comparison, however, is between *The Ox-Bow Incident* and the formula cowboy story, which is about as profitable as trying to find the meaning and excellence of *Moby Dick* by limiting yourself to a discussion of ways in which it does not fall into the clichés and ineptitudes of the formula sea story. Clark's critics have tried to analyze the novel by negation—the narrative is not loose, the cavalry (in this case, the sheriff) does not gallop unrealistically to the rescue—and the result is an impoverished criticism amounting to little more than praise for a tight, suspenseful narrative.[1] Placing a work of art in its proper genre is essential to criticism, but the discovery of that proper genre must itself be an act of criticism.

Certainly Clark chose the setting with reason. *The Ox-Bow Incident* is Western in a significant way, and its craftsmanship is excellent. The novel, however, cannot be called a cowboy story except in some perversely abstract sense, except in that sense in which *The Scarlet Letter* is a true-confessions story or *Hamlet* a detective-mystery. Nor can the injustice of lynch-law be called the subject of the novel, for surely the subject of a work of art must be something which is investigated. Hemingway's *A Farewell to Arms,* for example, includes an investigation of the subject of loyalty. Frederic Henry is a conscientious volunteer who deserts, and neither his devotion to duty nor his desertion is overtly condemned. The problem is subjected to esthetic study. But in *The Ox-Bow Incident* there is no evidence that lynching, under any circumstances, is just or even expedient. Most men consider lynching wrong, both legally and morally; and the novel does not question that judgment. It questions something else.

I   *The Intrinsic Question*

If the reader is not distracted by comparisons with the formula cowboy story or by the belief that the book is an allegorical warning against Nazi tyranny, he will find, I think, that the story itself suggests a quite different and much more rewarding set of questions.

Why does the novel begin and end with Art Croft and Gil Carter despite the fact that neither plays a major role in those events which are central to the novel? What is the relevance of the long gambling scene which opens the novel? What is the relevance of the discussion of Art and Gil's emotional problems built up on winter range? What sense are we to make of Davies, who seems the most admirably moral character in the novel and is yet allowed to disintegrate into pathetic helplessness? Why is

Gerald Tetley—the novel's second most articulate spokesman for morality—made to be so weak that he is disgusting to Art Croft, the narrator? Why does Clark spend so much time—in an economical novel—getting the lynchers started; and why is the lynching not stopped? If Davies' academic explanation is wrong, what is the answer? If he is right, how relevant are his finely drawn distinctions to the hardheaded realism which characterizes the tone of the novel?

II   An Everlasting Part of Things

The passages which give rise to these and to comparable questions share a common emphasis. Clark repeatedly focuses our attention on pent-up emotions and internal meanings, on the difficulty of giving external shape to the internal, and on the danger of fragmented projections of the inner self. In the opening paragraph, the land, not yet unpent from winter, is working its way out into spring. It is the same with Art Croft and Gil Carter, for "winter range stores up a lot of things in a man, and spring roundup hadn't worked them all out." [2] Once in the saloon, working off their "edge" with drinks and kidding, Art and Gil discover that the ranchers around Bridger's Wells are also pent-up, also on "edge," for someone has been stealing cattle. Gil joins a poker game and begins to win heavily, but "with his gripe on he [does not take] his winning right" (21); and Art begins to worry about Farnley, who "wasn't letting off steam in any way" (22). The scene becomes structurally relevant when Farnley does "let off steam" by becoming the symbolic leader of the lynch mob. The pattern continues with Major Tetley, the actual leader; and with Davies and Gerald Tetley, who are the voices of conscience; and with numerous minor characters: inner feelings must be projected into practical action, but there must be an alignment between the unconscious and the conscious if that projection is to be healthy. And there is the constant danger —in small matters as well as in the lynching—that what is inside man will be given a distorted projection; and the result will be a horror, at best a helplessness.

This value system, I think, underlies language and event throughout the novel; but it is given its most straightforward expression in a comparatively minor passage. Art Croft, almost parenthetically, offers a brief description of Kinkaid, the cowboy whose supposed death the lynchers want to avenge: "He was only an ordinary rider, with no flair to give him a reputation, but still there was something about him which made men cotton to him; nothing he did or said, but a gentle, permanent reality that was in him like his bones or his heart, that made him seem like an everlasting part of things"(36).

Kinkaid's character does not consist in deeds or words—that is, in either the pragmatic or the rational—but in some quality of "bones" and "heart" which expresses a sense of "permanent reality" and expresses it with balance and unity as "an everlasting part of things." These values, I hope to show, are comparable to those which C. G. Jung describes as archetypal. They are the property of the unconscious mind, and the rational mind— like that of Davies—finds itself incapable in their domain. The rational mind can comment and analyze, even with some validity; but it cannot project its ideas into action. It is possible for man to sense his alignment with archetypal reality, and then esthetically and ethically successful action may occur; but the rational mind cannot will a sense of "permanent reality" into the concrete events of human activity.

The American Dream, however, in direct opposition to Jungian principles, has emphasized individuality, which is both the price and privilege of democracy. As democracy releases man from cultural and political tyranny, individualism also begins to imprison man within the confines of his own temporal powers of creation. Too often, the emphasis on free will leads to an emphasis on ego and degenerates into greed and into an exaggerated evaluation of the male ego. Clark—again like Jung—holds that the male ego tends to separate man from the permanent, to distort projection. The intellect, also severed from the permanent, is associated with a degrading version of the feminine. Thus the lynch mob in *The Ox-Bow Incident* misappropriates for itself a monopoly on virtuous masculinity, and thus the protestations of Davies and Gerald Tetley are repeatedly associated —both in language and action—with a degrading femininity. But unlike Jung, Clark puts the archetypal to work in problems of American democracy; and he assigns to man's unconscious an ethical responsibility which is normally associated with the rational mind. Whether playing poker or joining a lynch mob, man is morally responsible for projecting his responsibility onto the human stage of action; and this projection, though it is properly subject to the judgments of the rational mind, cannot be generated by the rational mind. If man balks before the burden, if archetypal energies are betrayed by the fears or by the ambitions of the self-conscious intellect, terror is let loose.

III *Cheap Male Virtues*

Twenty-eight men, ostensibly led by Major Tetley, pursue, capture, and lynch three men believed to be guilty of cattle rustling and murder. During the pursuit, Gerald Tetley protests to Art Croft that he thinks their mission despicable. Gerald is a character type, the weak and sensitive son of a stern father and a doting mother. His father bullies him, demanding that he develop the pride of aggressive manhood. His mother, now dead, had always interceded to protect her son from a stern father and a cruel world. Having to face the Major by himself, Gerald is helpless and he is doomed. Yet what he says represents one extreme of a polarity essential to the structure of *The Ox-Bow Incident*.

Denouncing the "cheap male virtues" of physical courage (136), Gerald argues that all men fear the pack—the mass of society which bullies its members, forcing each person to become brutish rather than risk exposing to mass contempt his own inner tenderness and weakness. Each man has dreams; but, says Gerald, "nothing could make us tell them, show our weakness, have the pack at our throats" (137); and yet these dreams are true.[3] No man, Gerald continues, wants to hear the truth; no man wants to hear the confessor: "We're afraid that sitting there hearing him and looking at him we'll let the pack know that our souls have done that too, gone barefoot and gaping with horror, scrambling in the snow of the clearing in the black woods, with the pack in the shadows behind them" (138).

Gerald is uncomfortably right, and his rightness can be seen in emotional details which constitute the real cause behind the lynching of three innocent men. Even Art Croft, after hearing Gerald's confession, goads Gerald with the threat of "cheap male virtues": "I'm not wrong about your being here, am I?" (140). It is wrong for Art to question Gerald's loyalty to honest citizenship, to make him protest that he is not on the side of the rustlers; and Art knows it is wrong and feels "mean" to ask the question, but he does ask it. Clark's irony here is missed unless we remember that neither Art (who later admits to Davies that he felt all along that the lynching was wrong) nor Gil (who keeps remembering, though he is reluctant to confess it, an earlier hanging he had seen and been horrified by) wants to join the lynch mob. Both are participating in murder because they fear an inner reality. Both give in to society's divisive value system which associates virtue with a willingness to join the he-man lynch mob. Repeatedly, Art and Gil show themselves ready to fight with fists or with guns in order to show their allegiance to a cause in which they do not believe.

Jung, who describes the same fear, places it in the realm of the unconscious and thus in the domain of the archetypal. People, he explains, are "afraid of becoming conscious of themselves." [4] This fear, furthermore, is different from that reserve prompted by the good manners of one's society. "Beyond all natural shyness, shame and tact," Jung writes, "there is a secret fear of the unknown 'perils of the soul.' Of course one is reluctant to admit such a ridiculous fear." [5] Jung's explanation of the danger of "secret fear" is strikingly relevant to *The Ox-Bow Incident:*

> There is indeed reason enough why man should be afraid of those nonpersonal forces dwelling in the unconscious mind. We are blissfully unconscious of those forces because they never, or almost never, appear in our personal dealings and under ordinary circumstances. But if, on the other hand, people crowd together and form a mob, then the dynamics of the collective man are set free—beasts or demons which lie dormant in every person till he is part of a mob. Man in the crowd is unconsciously lowered to an inferior moral and intellectual level, to that level which is always there, below the threshold of consciousness, ready to break forth as soon as it is stimulated through the formation of a crowd. [6]

Man's unconscious, for Clark as for Jung, is both his hope for contact with archetypal reality and—when pent-up, when joined with mob-energy instead of with the energy of nature—the source of horror. As mentioned earlier, however, Clark believes man must learn to think through unconscious archetypes for the purpose of making ethical distinctions. We see this most obviously in Art Croft's reflections on Gerald's outburst:

> I realized that queerly, weak and bad-tempered as it was, there had been something in the kid's raving which had made the canyon seem to swell out and become immaterial until you could think the whole world, the universe, into the half-darkness around you: millions of souls swarming like fierce, tiny, pale stars, shining hard, winking about cores of minute, mean feelings, thoughts and deeds. To me his idea appeared just the opposite of Davies'. To the kid what everybody thought was low and wicked, and their hanging together was a mere disguise of their evil. To Davies, what everybody thought became, just because everybody thought it, just and fine, and to act up to what they thought was to elevate oneself. And yet both of them gave you that feeling of thinking outside yourself, in a big place; the kid gave me that feeling even more, if anything, though he was disgusting. You could feel what he meant; you could only think what Davies meant. (139)

Here are the central argument and the typical image of Clark's allegiance to American sacrality. Though Art Croft's sin, in a general way, is the same as Major Tetley's, he is an appropriate narrator for a sacred novel in that he is moving toward the acceptance of ethical responsibilities in a world of archetypal realities. He wants to think outside himself, to a reality more objective than the personal projections of the romanticized individualist. The objectively real, furthermore, must be felt— a requirement which suggests mysticism, or knowledge of the real apprehended by a means beyond human analysis. Gerald, however, in stressing the imaginative at the expense of the practical, disgusts Art, who does not like to see a man pour "out his insides without shame"; and Art admits also a deep admiration for Davies, whose intellectual and very unmystical approach also gives "that feeling of thinking outside yourself." Art Croft has thus accepted a Western version of the American paradox.

The universal principles of justice, as formulated and intellectualized by Davies, are not illusions. They represent a part of our history, and the American of integrity cannot take D. H. Lawrence's advice (given throughout his *Studies in Classic American Literature*) to ignore an ethical duty because it is not

honored with the ontological status that is the exclusive property
of the unconscious. Clark's hero is obligated to grant the rights
of the internal self, the ethical duties owed to others, and, unlike
his Eastern counterparts, to accept the primary reality of the
archetypes of the unconscious. He intellectualizes nervously (all
of Clark's heroes are painfully rational; none are mindless); he
is concerned with the practical world (law in *The Ox-Bow Incident*, adjustment problems from boyhood to manhood in urban
America in *The City of Trembling Leaves*, the settling of the
West in *The Track of the Cat*); and he realizes or comes to realize that the unconscious mind must be in tune with primordial
reality.

IV   *The Dramatic Shape of Ethical Reality*

The goal is not so much to find sacred unity in a profane time
as it is to live in that profane time without losing altogether one's
capacity for sacred unity. Rather than striving pathetically for
Nirvana on the plains, Clark's most sensible heroes hope more
modestly just to keep in touch. Thus the practical function of
sacrality is usually in the form of a reminder, a warning, a hint
that restores perspective. Neither the mystical nor the intellectual, certainly, can lead to unity. Throughout Clark's works, mystical and unusually sensitive characters are either disgusting,
like Gerald, or ineffectual, like Arthur in *The Track of the Cat*.
The intellectual, like Davies, is sympathetic but ineffectual; and
the intellect—when associated with the coolness of a Major
Tetley—tends toward cruelty and self-destruction. Unity, which
Clark associates with balance, cannot be achieved by a narrow
personality.

The Reverend Osgood, for example, is right intellectually,
and, according to Art, sincere; but he fails as a man and as a
minister. The fact that his advice to the lynchers is legal, ethical,
and sensible is irrelevant. His words do not spring from the generative unconscious, and thus they come stillborn into the world
of action and make men turn away, ashamed. Osgood, of course,
is not a whole man. He represents man's cowardly severance
of parts from a whole he is neither humble enough nor brave
enough to sense. This severance, quite understandably, is for
Clark an ugly operation. The severed part is still there, dangling;

but the victim pretends the damaged part does not exist. The sense of the whole must be felt with such courage and conviction that it results in a projection which has an honest face, which is dramatically effective.

Osgood's failure, therefore, is described in esthetic terms. Since his position obligates him to stop the lynching, the Reverend tries; but he goes about it "busily, as if he didn't want to, but was making himself" (41). His intellectual concept of an official duty cannot give birth to genuine emotion or action. His efforts are fragmented: he starts, and then stops, unable to get going, unable to speak with force or persuasion, incapable even of persuading himself. (The lynch mob has excessive energy, but it is distorted mob-energy, repugnant to man's ethical sense; and thus the mob too starts and stalls, has difficulty getting under way.) He waves his hands, nervously, thrusts them in his pockets again, and looks, at one point, "as if he were going to cry" (40). Art notices that his "bald head was pale in the sun," that the "wind fluttered his coat and the legs of his trousers," that he "looked helpless and timid" (41). His voice "was too high from being forced"; and, Art concludes, "He talked with no more conviction than he walked" (41).

Osgood, as a man, is embarrassing, which is not to say that brave men have a full head of hair or that men with high voices are cowards. Clark has chosen to describe Osgood's pathetic, ineffectual efforts in esthetic terms because he is concerned with the necessity of the archetypal source. Osgood, who flutters his hands as a nervous reaction to his own incompetence, speaks in a voice "too high from being forced" because his source is his own sterile will instead of the energizing archetypes of the unconscious. He has given himself over to officialdom's grotesque separation of man from the totality to which he belongs. He has alienated himself from that essential unity of thought and things, and a spiritually truncated man is a disgusting sight to behold.

This alienation, I think, explains why Clark begins the novel with a brief study in restoration. Though close friends, Art and Gil have succumbed to the tension of winter range; and they have argued and fought. They must now ease out of their divisive feelings, but the restoration can take place only if there is a sense of balance, a sense of the whole. They do not "dare talk much," and they are eager "to feel easy together again" (4). The

clipped and ironic conversation, the mask of jokes to cover a bitterness which must not be allowed to grow, and the ritual of restraint represent a sense of the whole of which Osgood is una-
ware.

Art and Gil's entrance into Bridger's Wells, with its suggestions of rites of passage, is immediately contrasted with Monty
Smith, whose degraded insensitivity makes him one of the most
despicable villains in Clark's archetypal world. A "soft-bellied,
dirty fellow," he wears a "half-shaved beard with strawberry
patches showing through, sore and itchy" (5). Though opposite
Davies and Gerald, though worse even than Osgood, he too is
an embarrassment. He is a sponge, the town bum, and he cheap-
ens manliness by pretending to be a genuine cowboy able to buy
a round of drinks in turn. Gil is too much a man of feelings to
be an ideal Clark hero, but he does feel with a roughhouse type
of honesty; and the certainty that Monty Smith will try to sponge
a drink makes him "sore." He reins his horse sharply, and Art
says, "Take it easy" (6). Gil does not reply, nor does he tell Art
what he feels. Art has enough insight (he is apparently a writer)
to know what his partner feels, and both have at least some
ability to think through things.

Inside Canby's saloon, Art and Gil begin to drink. Behind the
bar is a large and ludicrous oil painting entitled "Woman with
Parrot," but called by Canby himself "The Bitching Hour." The
painting shows a large woman, half-draped, lounging, holding
a parrot. Behind the woman appears a man who seems to be
sneaking up on her, or perhaps he is being lured by the woman
to his destruction. Gil complains that the man "is awful slow
getting there" and thinks the woman "could do better" (8).
Canby defends the man, who is always "in reach and never able
to make it." He thinks the woman has a "mean nature" (8).

The painting, it seems to me, makes an ironic comment on the
major action. The tension in the painting is frozen, caught for
all time; and the style is melodramatic, unrealistic. The tensions
of the real world, by contrast, must be resolved in action. Almost
every character in the novel, at one time or another, feels un-
manned or at least that his manhood is doubted. Because of the
high value placed on the male ego (even Ma ranks high in the
cult), tension is built up; and banked emotions demand satisfaction, gross or otherwise. Tyler and Osgood swell around, pa-

thetically trying to assert their authority. A feeble old man and
an irate woman tongue-lash the reluctant lynchers. Smith, as
a fraud, finds his manhood constantly in jeopardy, specifically
when he must bum a drink from Art and then leaves, "hitching
his belt in the doorway to get his conceit back" (11); and it is
this need which makes him eager to participate in the lynching.
Even Gil is unsettled from having lost his girl, an unmanly thing
to do; and Major Tetley, of course, is determined to prove both
his own manly leadership and the courage of his son. In general,
the ability of the ranchers of Bridger's Wells to protect their
own cattle is in question. As a result of these small and large
distortions, the lynching occurs.

This, I think, is the relevance of the opening scene, one instance in which resolution takes place with a sense of the whole,
and the means to a better understanding of the entire novel.
During the banter about the painting, Art reflects that Gil and
Canby "said something like this everytime we came in. It was
a ritual" (8). And the word "ritual," of course, suggests that unconscious realities are being shaped into the world of actuality.
It is with ceremonial implications, then, that Art takes his cue
from Canby, whose "face stayed as set as an old deacon's" (10),
and begins describing the fight he had with Gil. Ironic and
friendly insults are then swapped by Art and Gil. Gil justifies
having knocked Art across a red-hot stove by saying a man has
to have exercise. Art, he complains, is not much of a fighter, "but
there wasn't anything else handy" (19). Art counters by kidding
his partner's inept singing. They are "talking off" their "edge,"
and Canby puts "in a word now and then to keep [them] going" [7] (11). The tension built up during winter range cannot be
ignored, nor should it be allowed its natural expression. It must
be shaped.

V *Unity: The Poker Game and the Lynching*

The ethical, therefore, stands in a curious relation to the esthetic. There are qualities and shades of qualities. Clark's vision,
I think, reveals reason and feeling as neither good nor bad. What
is desired is unity, a sense of the whole, with reason and feeling
in their proper place, that is, with feeling (or the unconscious)
as man's contact with reality while reason serves as man's con-

scious recording device for what the unconscious has taught.[8] Davies, after all, pleads for feeling more than for reason. He is not the cold intellectual without heart. His failure is in his effort to make the rational do the work of the unconscious and in his resultant inability to give his beliefs the shape of dramatic conviction, which is not to imply that Clark has stooped to formulas.

Certainly Major Tetley is a master performer, and his ability to control the lynching party is an actor's ability. He speaks to a man without looking at him—holding his own face full camera —and thus keeps "inferiors" in their place. He knows when to pause, how to ignore an opponent, when to turn rebellion by a soft reply. He is cunning, an archetypal characteristic of pent-up and distorted energies. As the master of male ego, he is the natural leader. Gil Carter, for example, offended by Farnley's accusations at the card table, rouses his manliness and knocks Farnley flat. Offended by Major Tetley, he again asserts his manhood, fully prepared for a gunfight, only to be turned into helplessness by Major Tetley's quiet sophistry. Gil is left in the frustrated position of feeling right but looking wrong, which happens, in different ways, to Osgood, Davies, and Gerald, and which happens also, in the climax of the novel, to the three victims of the lynching.

The lynching is, psychologically and structurally, a culmination, a terrible increase of numerous minor injustices which occur throughout the novel and which are enacted according to the same ground rules that permit murder. The long poker game is a direct preparation for what takes place at the Ox-Bow. Gil begins to win, but he does not win in the right way. He neither apologizes nor gloats. Rather, he rakes in the pot as if he expected it. And Farnley, the heaviest and most disgruntled loser, also refuses to play the game right when he calls for double draw, even though he is not dealing, even though double draw is not "real poker." The judgments made after their fight are made by the same code, except this time Gil does it right. Canby knocks Gil out with a bottle, and then starts to take his gun. Art shakes him off. He knows his buddy, and his buddy will take it in the right way, and that he does, coming out of it slow but joking. There is a right way to play poker and a wrong way, a right way to fight and a wrong way. One of the final comments in the novel is Gil's statement that he will not fight the sophisti-

cated dude who took his girl. "I don't know how to start a decent fight with that kind of a guy" (287), he says, and readers
will be reminded of Art's hope, just before the lynching, that
Martin would "make the decent end he now had his will set on"
(240). The Mex, who has held center stage and earned the admiration of everyone by removing a bullet from his own leg,
spits in contempt when old Hardwick buckles, saying ironically,
"This is fine company for a man to die with" (243). But in the
end the Mex goes to pieces and screams, talking "panicky in
Spanish" (246); and Art comments: "In the pinch Martin was
taking it the best of the three" (246). How to die, how to fight,
how to play poker, how to stop a lynching: all are studies in the
same world view.

After it has become known that the three hanged men are
innocent, Davies flagellates himself, embarrassing Art with a
destructive confession. Davies does make some valid points—
his denunciation of the sins of omission, for example—but his
confession is repugnant because it comes from a part-man. Art,
though enough of a moral coward to confine his opposition to
"safe" actions like the fetching of Judge Tyler, though he puts
aside his conscience and does not vote to delay the hanging,
is a more complete being than Davies. His insight into people
characterizes the novel, and he has at least some contact with
the unity of all things; but he is also remarkably acute in reading the motives of Davies' rational will. He does miss Davies
from time to time, but his understanding of the rational mind
is a mark of Clark's American revision of Jungian archetypes.

That revision is a fairly complex one. It is certainly bold. By
what guilt or fate, then, have twenty-eight men come to the
horror of lynching three innocent men? Clark's answer—or the
closest thing to it for an author who feels that questions are
more legitimate than answers—[9] is his dramatization of the horrors of divisive lives. It is contained in the portraits of Judge
Tyler and the Reverend Osgood and in the obscene ethic of their
narrow little roles as half-men; in the tough sentimentality of
Ma and the shocking result of her eagerness to do a man's job;
in the bumbling but honest frustrations and high-jinks of Gil
Carter; in the sympathetic obsession of Davies' doomed but
honorable intellectualism; in the embarrassing but insightful
confession of the girl-man Gerald Tetley; and even in the melo-

dramatic tyranny of Major Tetley, the master play-actor of male ego.

The reality which lies behind the archetypal ethic of *The Ox-Bow Incident* is a reality one apprehends best by belonging as an "everlasting part of things." [10] Man does not achieve his real self in idea or office or emotion, but as an individual part of a larger whole. Man's only hope is to act from a sense of the integrity of that larger eternity, and his most shocking failure is to murder innocent men on behalf of his own dedication to a severed piece of man called the male ego. When that failure occurs, his victim will be most probably a man like Martin, an innocent, naïve in the affairs of the manly world, the natural prey of the mob-beast that grows from man's neglected unconscious.

The subject of *The Ox-Bow Incident*, I have tried to suggest, is not a plea for legal procedure. The subject is man's mutilation of himself, man's sometimes trivial, sometimes large failures to get beyond the narrow images of his own ego. The tragedy of *The Ox-Bow Incident* is that most of us, including the man of sensitivity and the man of reason, are alienated from the saving grace of archetypal reality. Our lives, then, though not without possibility, are often stories of a cruel and irrevocable mistake.

CHAPTER *4*

Ironic Sacrality: *The City of*
Trembling Leaves

WALTER Clark's second novel, *The City of Trembling Leaves*, was so unlike the first that it confused the critics. *The Ox-Bow Incident* had been tense, controlled, dramatic. Its story was exciting and of obvious importance to man in society. But in *The City of Trembling Leaves* Clark seemed to have lost that tight control which had characterized his initial success. The second novel was said to be episodic, drawn out, and unresolved. The materials too were judged to be ill-chosen, consisting of high school tennis matches and track meets, adolescent love affairs, a naked swim in which nothing happened though Clark clearly felt the scene to be central to his structure, and various narrative and lyrical passages on hero Tim Hazard's career as a musician. Even the tone was found to be uncontrolled —shifting without discoverable reason—and the novel as a whole seemed undercut by a juvenile rationale and by themes which did not arrive anywhere.

Clark's reviewers, with his second novel as with his first, were taking an extrinsic approach. Their concern with Clark's career —rather than with his novel—led them to ask questions that were minor or irrelevant: Was *The City of Trembling Leaves* written before *The Ox-Bow Incident* but published afterwards? Does this explain the immaturity of the second novel in contrast with the mature craftsmanship of the first? Is Tim Hazard an autobiographical portrait Clark put together to satisfy some personal need? [1] I did not ask Clark to answer these questions, but he posed them voluntarily as questions typical of interviews, and his answers need to be quoted in full:

No—*The City of Trembling Leaves* was not written before *Ox-Bow* and published later. That assumption, I think—and the question has been put to me often—arises from another equally incorrect assumption—that the book is intensely autobiographical —and was just one of those things every young writer has to get out of his system. Another reaction—common to nearly all the reviewers—whether they liked the book or not—arose from those assumptions, I believe—that *City* was a loose, picaresque novel, a mere loose, sequential accumulation of remembered experiences. . . . I did make several bad passes at something like *The City* before I wrote *Ox-Bow*—but the book that was printed was a complete reconception, and no part of it was written before *Ox-Bow*. Nor is it anything like as autobiographical as has been generally assumed.[2]

Clark's polite impatience with his reviewers is justified. I would say myself that *The Track of the Cat* is his best novel and that *The Ox-Bow Incident* is second; but *The City of Trembling Leaves* is a very good novel: it is ordered, and its structure and tone have not yet been analyzed. Certainly, the novel was misunderstood and, therefore, inadequately reviewed. One of the main causes of the misreading is the non-Western American's unfamiliarity with sacrality. The other main cause—involving the large question of Western stylistics—has been the object of scholarly quests for over thirty years and cannot be neatly handled here as a minor part of this chapter, but a few remarks on the subject are prerequisite to an analysis of *The City of Trembling Leaves.*

I *The Stylistics of American Sacrality*

A sacred vision calls for a style like that of the Japanese Haikai, a style that uses the senses to evoke a meaning which is profound and which is not subject to conscious analysis.[3] This distinction is more than the usual one between the logic of criticism and the non-logic of art. It is as if the medium itself were different, as if the Haikai were a painting, a form of art using a medium different in kind from words. The Haikai, as well as other illustrative forms like the haiku and hokku, is highly stylized and depends for its existence on a rather elaborate tradition. It is the tradition, perhaps as much as the artistry of the sense-paintings, which enables the Haikai to escape the merely private and to become communicable art.

If those Western writers who are attracted to sacrality lived in a culture with a set of traditions comparable to those of Japan, they too would create an art that would seem non-verbal, that would evoke immediately the responses of the primal self. But American traditions, far from inviting forms like that of the Haikai, are antagonistic to literary art that aims toward the non-verbal. American traditions—whether conservative, liberal, or Western—are fundamentally committed to practicality, realism, consciousness, the conscience, and to the responsibilities of the individual as a reasoning ego with ethical duties. Though my strategy here may seem perverse, too dependent on a merely expedient hypothesis, it has the advantage, I think, of making sense of a confusion of possibilities. The style of the sacred Westerner, I am suggesting, would be different in kind from other styles if he lived in a country which provided the necessary traditions. As a sacred man born to a profane culture, he is loyal to his profane history and yet attracted to non-verbal art; and thus he is a conscious and verbal artist who uses non-verbal techniques when he thinks they can be made to work.

Although bold and sometimes successful efforts in Orientalist evocation are made, the results are for the most part a difference in degree rather than in kind. Both the sacred and the non-sacred American, after all, must appeal to the conscious and to the unconscious. The sacred writer is realistically aware of his place in a profane history, and non-sacred writers (those who are friendly to sacrality, of course, writers like Melville and Hemingway, but also naturalists like Dreiser and Norris, conservatives like Eliot and Cozzens) are aware of the primal fears and urges within all men and are able, at times, to create a sense of the primal for their readers. The differences in degree that occur do not lend themselves to neat generalizations.

Two differences, however, do hold, at least as far as Clark is concerned. First, when a non-sacred writer tries to tap the unconscious directly and to bypass the rational as a mode of apprehension, as anything but a mode of reflection after the act of reading, he tends to provide some stylistic shibboleth as tribute to the primary authority of the rational mind. He will signal the change. As a cinema which switches from the actual to the imaginative will use music or distortion or montage to signal that

fidelity to the actual is being dropped, so will the non-sacred
novelist tend to use stylistic devices to make it clear to the reader
that, for a time, he is dealing in abnormal materials.

Hawthorne, for example, was especially sensitive on this point
and could seldom resist the compulsion to intrude as author and
to apologize, to voice disclaimers. A favorite device is to switch
to the viewpoint of a questionable or superstitious observer. Melville's interest in the primordial was not so timid, yet no one
can miss the sudden change in the weather of Melville's atmosphere when Fedallah appears aboard the *Pequod.* The signals,
with or without apologies, are there. This does not mean that
the primal for Melville or even for Hawthorne is unreal—far
from it. The point is that Clark, who believes the unconscious
to be primary to the conscious, who believes that the sacred and
the profane are signs of man's inadequacy to *be* and not signs
of ontological dualism, feels no compunction to offer a signal,
no need to distinguish in stylistic terms between the truth of
reason and the truth of archetypal response. The reviewers of
The City of Trembling Leaves, I think, were not disturbed by
Clark's delving into sacred realities so much as by his refusing
to testify in his style to the primary authority of the rational
mind, to his refusal to make stylistic apologies when shifting his
subject from tennis matches to mountain sprites.

The second generalization I am willing to risk is especially
relevant to a reading of *The City of Trembling Leaves.* There is
a critical bias today favoring those writers whose style is consistent enough and distinct enough that it becomes a recognizable
voice, like that of Twain, Hemingway, or Faulkner. Clark, as
discussed earlier (see the conclusion of Chapter Two), feels that
each work should be unique, not just in the sense that a work
of art has boundaries, borders, an integrity, but in the sense that
each work should have its own style, its own voice. In *The City
of Trembling Leaves* Clark has gone even further in that he employs at least five distinct styles: lyric, dramatic, ironic, satiric,
and farcical. Variety is, of course, a characteristic of art; but
Clark's radical shifts of stylistic personality have run counter to
the critical tone of the present day. The critic's emphasis on
consistency, development, progress—esthetic assumptions related
to the cultural dictum advising men to get somewhere, and re-

lated also to the cultural emphasis on cause-and-effect progress in linear time—has led to the conclusion that Clark is an artist in search of something he cannot find.

But, for the writer whose world view is cosmogonic, seeing experience in terms of cause and effect as understood by the rational mind is a violation of the sacred reality of human existence. When such a writer lives in a country with social, political, and religious beliefs that are cosmologically oriented, then a fairly definite and peaceful separation can be made between the sacred act and the profane act. When he lives in a profane democracy, however, he must shape his cosmology as best he can wherever he can; and thus for writers like Clark and Steinbeck experience which a primitive could be content to call profane must be potentially sacred. The style of an artist of sacrality, then, is atypical in that it may blend, without signals, an ordinary weekend mountain climb and a sacred mountain climb, in that it may blend the irony of history with the sacrality of the universe without a shift in viewpoint. Since all experience is felt to adhere in ultimate unity, no violence is done the sacred sensibility by a style which multiplies possibilities beyond the patience of a reader committed to reason and to the conscious intuition. An experience may relate to another by community membership in cosmic unity or by those cause-and-effect relationships which characterize the expectations of a typical reader.

Clark's style, then, is built to accommodate the emotive wiles of the subject at hand. He has not been concerned to develop a consistent voice, and he has not been afraid of imitation. In *The Track of the Cat*, for example, Clark uses "so" in a Faulknerian fashion (388) and "now" in the manner of Hemingway (331), but he also writes a passage which is so like Stephen Crane—both in form and content—that it sounds like plagiarism. Curt has been pursuing the black painter, but he is beginning to crack, and he is coming to feel that *he* is the pursued:

> The most important single fact in the world was again the fact that cats can see in the dark. He resented bitterly the fact that cats could see in the dark. It seemed to him that the malicious and chancy god of things had enabled cats to see in the dark for the sole purpose of rendering this already unequal hunt even more unequal. Often, as he crouched, he felt very sorry for himself, and wondered at the enormous indifference of a universe

which could permit a tragedy of these proportions to be enacted before no audience but trees and stars. (338)[4]

This variety of styles does not mean that Clark is in search of something he cannot find but that he wants to avoid style as a preconception, dictating to the material, that he seeks the style required by the material. His use of a Stephen Crane style in the above passage, for example, is appropriate in that Curt, at that point, senses the collapse of his pompously unrealistic values and feels that sophomoric petulance before indifferent "trees and stars" which is so characteristic of the condition of Crane heroes.

The ironically pedantic style of "The Writer and the Professor" is recurrent throughout Clark, especially in *The City of Trembling Leaves*; and yet he is capable of using folk-talk (unsuccessfully, I think) to take the taint from a line felt to be improperly intellectual: "He couldn't stand getting reined down logical" (*The Ox-Bow Incident*, 59). Clark's aim in all cases is that of the supreme organicist: he seeks the form that is inherent in his materials. *The Ox-Bow Incident*, as a novel about a climactic event in the profane world, is structured in terms appropriate to linear time. *The City of Trembling Leaves*, as a novel of adventures into the sacred world, is structured in terms appropriate to cyclical time.

II   *The Ersatz Jungle*

The definitive characteristic of a sacred man—whether in the Orient or in the American West—is his belief that the generative source of energy and the authority for ontology are in the original creation of the universe.[5] If man can unify himself with the original, he can tap the energies that are latent within all men; if he will permit himself to sense the multiple gods of creation, he can align his soul with the wondrous variety of the universe. But men who attempt to drive themselves by the bastard energies of a nervous intellect, who attempt to restrict creation to the simplistic limits of the rational mind, find themselves cut off from the generative source and imprisoned within the barrenness of rationality. *The City of Trembling Leaves* is a study of a sacred youth who lives in a profane age. The story is an epic initiation, too long and populous for a neat summary; but the main characters are Tim Hazard, the hero; Mary, his true and childhood sweetheart; Rachel, his idealized and impossible sweetheart; and Lawrence Black, an artist who makes a fatal bargain for uncommercialized purity. Clark traces Tim's growth from childhood to young manhood, and it is a story, primarily, of spiritual growth in a moribund city.

A city is moribund, it is explained in the "Prelude," when there are no trees, that is, when man's commercial and narrowly practical interests have invested his life with concrete and with "improved" real estate, when his values have lost touch with the original. A city without trees is emblematic of man's "drawing out of . . . alliance with the eternal," and such a withdrawal "will also choke out the trees in the magic wilderness of the spirit." [6] Reno, Nevada, Tim Hazard's home town, lying between two mountain ranges, enjoys a physical reminder of the eternal, and thus "the vigor of the sun" (the original energy) is strong enough to move men born to concrete and to commerce, strong enough to prompt the sacred growth of a Tim Hazard.

The narrator, later named as Walt Clark, explains that the purpose of the "Prelude" is "to celebrate" neither "newness as such" nor "oldness as such" (6). Like Whitman, narrator-Clark holds that "Temporal age is unimportant" (6). The point is that man needs to be "more open to the eternal and reproductive old" (6), to the generative primordial, outside temporal time, represented by the sacred mountains of Nevada. The average man "feels death coming on all the time, and, having no faith in reproduction or multiplicity, tries to build a fort to hold it off" (6). This "fort" is material wealth, or principally, for most of us, our houses; but houses are "incipiently evil [if they are] intended to master time and dominate nature" (6). This evil is, in the terms of Mircea Eliade's *Cosmos and History*, the fatal commitment to linear time,[7] a commitment Clark calls "moribund" because it is a commitment to that which is dying rather than an opening of one's self to that which is regenerative. For residents of Reno, the supreme instance of the moribund is downtown Reno, the famous part, "the ersatz jungle, where the human animals, uneasy in the light, dart from cave to cave under steel and neon branches . . ." (12).

III *The Irony of Sacred Unity*

The attack on materialism is so widespread in America that it is unlikely to result in more than a categorical nod from readers, but Clark attacks materialism in the name of sacrality; and this, apparently, has so stunned readers accustomed to believing in reason's sovereign control of reality that inadequate attention has been given to the strongest characteristic of *The City of Trembling Leaves.* The novel is, from first to last, ironic. Clark's sacred hero is the sacred fool, and his misadventures are consistently handled with an irony which becomes at times satiric and even, near the end, farcical.

Reviewers simply do not expect irony from a man who believes in "sprites." Even a casual glance at the chapter titles, however, reveals Clark's ironic strategy. The titles represent the voice of the narrator, and they stand in ironic relation to the misadventures of Tim Hazard. Seventeen include the word "about" and fifteen begin with the words "in which," suggesting satire of the type associated with the eighteenth century in England, as in the novels of Henry Fielding. The titles are long, usually, and the characteristic tone is lofty, comic, pompous, constituting an ironic commentary on sacred escapades too many readers have taken literally. Chapter 3, "About Divine Mary, and the Pagan Goddess Who Taught Art, and Jacob the Terrible Fiddler," deals with a pre-adolescent infatuation, with Tim's schoolboy fascination before an art teacher who wears jewelry and has an attractive figure, and with Jacob, a schoolboy who tries to become a concert violinist, but lacks a true musical ear, and commits suicide. Chapter 8, "About the Ceremony of Manhood Which Prepared Timothy Hazard for His Great Single Love," describes a schoolboy initiation, a battle royal in which the sophomores annually trounce the freshmen.

The ironic tone of these and other chapter titles, a tone developed in the novel itself, suggests that it is not Clark but his reviewers who have lost perspective about the place and importance of childhood and adolescence. The tone has been missed, apparently, by reviewers who come to a Western novel with James Fenimore Cooper in their heads or with visions of *ubi sunt* on the range. More germane, if comparisons are necessary, is

Herman Melville's *Pierre,* in which Melville mocks that which
he loves, the "fool of virtue" whose struggles against a harsh
reality are absurd, but whose absurdity is far more admirable
than the prestige-wisdom of those who accept the defeat of the
human spirit out of deference to factualist realism.

The central image of Tim's absurd sacrality, music, is not altogether successful. Both music and painting—and especially the
specific works named and described throughout the novel—leave
the reader feeling that too much is being asked of him, that he
is expected to respond to a song he cannot hear, to a painting he
cannot see. The importance of art to the characters, however, is
clear, as is the basic intent. Clark is seeking some form of the
Haikai, some image beyond words, a sense of unity which is non-
verbal and yet American and therefore realistic. Clark's concern
with absolutist sacrality, as in "Chuang tse, and the Prince of the
Golden Age," is merely sportive. The sacred unity he seeks is,
be it remembered, an Americanized version, a consciously realistic and therefore ironic version. The analogy between music and
the story of Tim Hazard is that music, like life, must be apprehended in parts, in linear time, yet is real only as a complete
whole. Man lives in pieces, lives in the minutes of the given day
a life which is real only insofar as he attains to unity.

It is for this reason that Clark describes in such detail Tim's
schoolboy days. Clark's sacred man lives neither in India nor
within some tomb of his inner self. He plays tennis, works in his
front yard, loves his woman, is bound and most willingly bound
to this earth and to its domesticity. That the sacred man needs
food, that he sweats, that he can lust absurdly for a curved and
bejeweled and perfumed body and be comically ignorant even
of his own lust, that he is *man,* in short, need not define his total
self or obfuscate his sacred self. That primordial reality which is
beyond words, which is invoked by Tim in wordless prayer and
in bursts of spontaneous musical creations, is inexorably real. The
rough edges of everyday realism, then, are not to be ignored or
even overcome. In fact, a somewhat trivial and certainly a social
rather than a metaphysical or religious "ceremony" prepares Tim
Hazard for his one Great Love. The sacred man is in love with
practical life or he is not sacred. He can even appreciate material
goods with impunity. His problems are not socio-economic or

even philosophical, for he has heard the archetypal speak; and
the voice of authority is difficult to deny. His problem is one of
alignment. He must feel himself in contact with a reality which
is beyond words, yet remember always that the particulars he
feels are the concrete objects of the world of nature and domesticity. "Shape" and "balance" are Clark's two favorite words for
this alignment, both suggesting an emphasis on the intuitive and
non-verbal capabilities of the unconscious. There is, it must be
remembered, no final, no fixed shape. Man moves in linear time,
and he is realistically conscious of so doing. Shape is temporary;
balance is something achieved for the moment, for this time.
There is no answer and no set procedure to absolve man from
the responsibility of trying to sense *this day* the non-verbal para-
digms of his existence.

Obviously, the writer who talks of discovering sacred unity in
the muck of daily multiplicity is a man who runs the risk of being
patently ridiculous. It is a risk Clark accepts. It is a challenge
Tim Hazard seems to have been given at birth. The irony of
this challenge, however, lies only partly in the disunity of the
real and the actual—a disunity which is more psychologically
destructive for the conscious hero than for the sacred hero. The
primary cause of irony is that sacrality tempts the believer to
dreams of perfection, and this temptation—which represents the
chief psychological danger of the sacred man—is the subject of
The City of Trembling Leaves.

In high school, Tim goes out for track and becomes the rival
of Red, who is the school's best runner and the sweetheart of a
pretty girl much admired by Tim. In the big race, the competition
between the two schools is less important than the contest between Tim and Red; and that contest, in turn, is less important
than the battle of Tim within himself. His problem includes necessarily the materials of this world, but the real contest is the
alignment of self with primordial reality. And alignment is so
much a personal matter that free will, for the sacred writer, is
scarcely relevant. Tim's natural running style, associated in his
mind with the "wild stallion," is symbolic of that balance which
is so essential to a realization within one's self of an alignment
with the eternal. In the moment of competition, however, Tim
cannot attain the rhythm of the stallion. The urge to overtake Red

is a consciousness which precludes the desired state, a state which must *occur*. There is no "release" in his run; it is a "working run" (193).

Later in the race, he begins to get it right: "He concentrated on evenness, and gradually the tension passed from him. A kind of golden anger of triumph poured into him. Second wind it is generally called, and it is made up as much of smoothness, of getting the inner and the outer runner together, as it is of attaining an oxygen balance. Joyously he thought, several times, rapidly and in the tempo of his running, 'Now I've got you' " (193–94). Having once achieved the state of balance, there is no "silly stride to think about, no miserish idea to cherish, like that of running evenly" (194). Easily, Tim wins the race. The outer man and the inner man have been made one. He is thus beyond ideas *about* running and has achieved the thing-in-itself of running.

The end of the episode, furthermore, suggests meanings far beyond those of the typical novel of adolescence and sports. Tim's team loses the track meet because of the personal competition between Tim and Red, and Red seems defeated as a person, not merely as a runner. Tim feels finally "as if he had cheated Red . . . as if he had cheated" the girl they both admired (197). Clark's subject is not high school track meets and the adventures of American youth. His subject is the temptation which lures toward destruction any man who has felt—with bone-knowledge, with blood-knowledge—his sacred self, the magic powers of the primordial. That temptation is the demon perfection.

IV   *A Utopia Made of Sand*

The profane man, by contrast, may be lured toward perfection only as a dim hope, only by the lure he himself is able to create out of his own will, his own self-determined notions of the perfect. The profane man, quite simply, has never felt the perfect in his stomach. His dreams are abstract, more a hope for some future day in linear time, some Eden at the end of a long drive. In a given day, he has little chance for an epiphany; his dreams of perfection are mental, and their strength has only the comparatively weak powers of his own imagination. The sacred man, by contrast, has not just dreamed of pure reality. He has touched

it. He has had the sacred experience which is felt-knowledge of
the real. His temptation to strive for perfection, then, is generated
by powers of primordial reality as confirmed by the unmistakable
touch of the living hand.

The sacred stone, Eliade emphasizes in his description of sacrality, is not a symbol of the real; it is the real.[8] That union of
the real and the actual which the profane man knows through
tenuous symbols is a union the sacred man may touch with his
hand at any time. The youthful Tim's experience of Christ and
church services is sadly typical of modern man: "he felt . . . as
if he were attending the funeral of someone he didn't know, and
was intent only on remaining inconspicuous so as not to offend
those who were really afflicted" (28–29). His experience of primordial reality, however, is typical only of those few who can
hear their own homunculus and know the wry and cheerful
doom of sacred life.

Such knowledge, the touch of the nuclear, is quite common for
the sacred man. It can come even in childhood, perhaps most
easily in childhood. Tim's childish "faith in ecstasy" (26) comes
frequently, though with frustrations, until he is seventeen. Before
his maturing experience with his dream-girl, Rachel Wells, he
prays every morning and every night and often several times
during the day. When his prayers become words or when they
take on a "fixed form" (27), they lose their power; and they are
dropped. His successful prayers, by contrast, are wordless: a
"mood which meant that, for a moment, he had touched what
God really was" (27). The experience, it should be emphasized,
is not mystical or transcendental, is not an illusion or a dream.
It is the actual touch of the real. For those who have had such
an experience, perfection is not an intellectual hope, an idle
dream. Perfection has been felt, and the magic of its touch cannot
easily be forgotten.

It is for this reason that critics are on dangerous ground when
they emphasize James Fenimore Cooper and *ubi sunt*. The theme
of a lost Garden of Eden and the theme of the everlasting frontier
are relevant to the West, but they are relevant for the most part
to minor and sentimental writers. In the more central tradition of
sacrality, perfection is not the exclusive property of yesteryear.
Homunculus does not live only on the frontier, nor has the arche-

typal lost its hegemony. Incapacitated man, it is true, has lost the courage to listen; but man's primal nature is still his primal nature, sidewalks and ulcers notwithstanding.

The City of Trembling Leaves is a story of primal nature in twentieth-century America. As such, it is the story of adolescent loves; of a painful growth toward mature love; of the wonder of sports and the pathos of family; and, most important, a story of the ancient quest for the golden answer. Clark recreates the smell of a schoolroom, the illusions and frustrations of a small boy's raunchy and holy nature, the sense of sacrality in a modern setting. Early in the novel, young Timmy, who dreams romantically of Tristram, is rudely awakened to another side of life: "Lucy and Gladys are gonna give out at noon hour, up in the jungle" (16–17). This boyishly lecherous announcement comes to Timmy with disturbing force. It taps something within him he is not sure he wants to have tapped. It disturbs, also, his budding pride; for he must pretend to worldly wisdom he does not yet possess. When Timmy thinks about his true sweetheart, Mary, it is "an act of devotion" (21)—pure and sexless.

To hear that two girls are going to "give out" is unsettling to Timmy even though he innocently asks, "Give out what?" (17). "Timmy had yet a long way to go," Clark explains, "before he discovered that he had an ego to maintain as a guide in all matters of moral confusion" (21). This association between ego and morality is important to our understanding of Clark's art. In his Americanization of Oriental thought, Clark has met our historical insistence on the democratic integrity of the individual ego and on the moral responsibilities of that ego. Timmy, in short, has sensed the wonder of the universe; but he has not learned to balance himself between the sovereign gods of the universe and the sovereign realities of the moral world.

On this score, at least, Clark may be compared with J. D. Salinger, whose Glass family juggling act is comparable to the balancing that goes on within Timmy; both writers also see their holy fools as being proper subjects for irony. Their characters' efforts, especially when immature, border on the ridiculous. In school, for example, Timmy fears that he may be called on to read; and his childish hope to avoid such a horror is indicative of his fantasy world: "He concentrated upon becoming invisible" (29). The significance of this hope is that it adumbrates later escapist tendencies: his love of Rachel, his fall into despair, his dreams of discovering the final answer through writing perfect music.

There is no escape, of course, not even in the schoolroom. Timmy is called on to read, and again a childish experience foretells the nature of adult experience. The rule of the classroom exercise is that a student will read only so long as he does not make a single mistake. One error means that he must sit down. Timmy, however, gets "caught" by the rhythm of *The Lady of the Lake* and reads flawlessly, no longer aware of himself or of the school rule, until the teacher is forced to stop him. The task here is comparatively simple, but the ground rules apply universally. To impose your person upon a poem, a girl, a piece of music, is to misread the poem, girl, or piece of music, and to lose one's holy self in the process. The reality of art and life and self can come only when man invokes the archetypal response, when he allows a natural integrity to speak through himself.

Such a response, I must emphasize, is not mindless. It is a way of knowing, a style of being that man's worship of fact and reason has placed in disrepute. Unlike the romantic (especially Wordsworth, Coleridge, and Shelley), who projects himself *onto* nature, Clark feels that nature should be projected *into* man. The romantic, like the immature Timmy, has not yet learned a condition of reality which applies to schoolboy reading, to sports, to love, to the creation of art, and to man's quest for the meaning of life itself. Since Timmy's sacred sensibilities are not yet tough enough, not yet attuned to harsh realities, his timid grasp of reality is undermined by the discovery that a "shiny, starchy girl like Dorothy" (43), a girl who seems as proper as his own worshipped Mary, is not beyond sex. When told that she "knows how to do it," that she "likes to do it" (43), he is shocked. The news shakes "the orderly autumn world into chaos" (43).

Despite his romanticism, his escapism into dreams, his illusions of perfection, Timmy is more hopefully launched than his brother Willis, whose cynical factualism has doomed him to live in a barren world, doomed him for the very simple reason that he is too "realistic" to see the magic of his own wilderness. For Clark, sacrality is more realistic than the reason, realism, and facts of those too blinded by moribund civilization to hear the voice of the archetypal. Even in his childhood, for example, Timmy re-

sponds as much to the indifference of nature as to its beauty, to
its terror as to its authority. For the orthodox Christian, the
weight of indifference felt before a mountain is a threat to belief;
similarly, the crying of devils up from the chambers of the inner
self is a threat to faith in man's own worthiness. For the sacred
man, there is a loss of the neatness of rational monotheism; but
there is also the very realistic advantage of holding to a vision
which accords more accurately with what he finds in nature and
within the inner self. Timmy is only a child, one of those "tiny
creatures upon the border of intellect" (49), but he feels "the
profound indifference to everything mortal which is part of a
planetary sense of time" (49); and thus his concept of God is
realistically related to the nature of existence. His concept of
multiple gods can accommodate the variety of powers he finds in
nature. This realistic grounding in sacrality makes it possible for
Timmy to become a man. His ability to hear the primal voice is
the means by which he can discipline himself to hear also the
voice of the intellect. The paradigm of his vision is archetypal
time, or timelessness, a major theme in the novel; and thus he is,
at bottom, more realistic than Willis, who can hear only the
incessant ticking of the clock.

Young Timmy, however, has not yet learned his way around in
the "magic wilderness." Sporting with Mary at Pyramid Lake,
he falls into a characteristic illusion: he feels sensations of a
marvelous unity with nature and with Mary. He feels "convinced
that this miracle of water, stone and light had been of his own
making, and that Mary also felt the new and marvelous splendor
of the wilderness that joined them" (57). His fantasy of the
sacred is of such thin stuff that it has no tolerance for the gibes
of Willis, whose mocking voice is "a choir of gnats and a cloud
of mosquitoes" (58); and a childish illusion of unity is shattered
by a childish voice of disunity.

In his boyhood friendship with Lawrence Black, Timmy under-
goes the same process. Both boys are neophytes in sacrality, as
shown by Tim's wordless prayers, pure extemporizing in music,
and ceremonial dances, and by Lawrence's creative talent with
his symbolically primal turtles and by his quaintly formal manners. Immature sacrality, and this is typical of Clark's vision, lures
them toward illusions of perfection; and they build a utopia,
made, significantly, of sand. To discuss the utopia, however, turns

out to be easier than to build it: the sand does not pack right, and their towers keep crumbling down. Timmy's romantic sacrality is also jeopardized by a lizard that carries a toad in his mouth and by Willis, the omnipresent pest, who spies on Timmy's girl, sees her "bare nakedy" (55), and boasts of it to Timmy.

Of such vague and petty lusts, such dreamings after reality, and such ceremonies in frustration, boyhood is made. The meanness is all of a kind: the cruel and casual shattering of innocence, the prematurely developed sixth-grade girl who teases male purity, the hot-eyed and panting boys who innocently destroy innocence because they cannot take their eyes off bosom and thigh or think of anything more real than doing wicked things in a restroom, in the bushes, around a corner from moralizing adults. Timmy's dreams, unrealistically, are, in the years before his teens, dreams of the abstract. It is ceremony he worships, not discovery; it is idealized nature he worships, and idealized nature does not permit the mouthing of toads by cruel lizards. Love in the abstract tantalizes him, and he finds that daydreams of love about Mary cannot lead to culmination but must veer away into ethereal generalizations. Sex is something you do with a girl like Lucy, or rather, dream of doing.

It is in such patterns, furthermore, that Clark develops his themes, builds a progression his reviewers did not perceive, for Timmy begins to change: "Timmy's transition from Mary, the worshipful symbol of all womankind, to Rachel, a personal deity, was assisted by other changes and events, which combined to lead him from the sunny fringe of the wilderness into its shadowy and more complicated depths" (86).

V *Lessons in Maturity: The Birth of the World*

Timmy's early childhood on "the sunny fringe of the wilderness" occupies, roughly, the first third of Book I. During this stage in his development, his image of himself is that of a character in his own fantasies, capable of dreamlike metamorphosis at the convenience of a childish need or whim. During the second third of Book I, Timmy becomes Tim; and he finds his dreams unwillingly anchored to a developing ego, an inescapable awareness of himself as an individual. The change from Mary to Rachel, like the worship of athletics, like the seminal incident of the moss agate, suggests that he has not yet learned to think through things, that he still dreams of imposing his sacred fantasies upon the actual world; but during this stage Tim begins to feel the power of the nuclear, and this beginning awareness marks his progress toward manhood.

The materials of his maturation, again, are realistic to the American scene. The physical stuff of Tim's world is domestic, commonplace. Chapter 8, for example, which is called "About the Ceremony of Manhood Which Prepared Timothy Hazard for His Great Single Love," is just as ironic as the title suggests. The "Ceremony" is an annual high school initiation rite, a mass brawl between the freshmen and the sophomores. During the battle, Timmy loses consciousness of himself in a kind of temporary insanity, a fury of selfless devotion to an absurd cause. His class loses, despite his maniacal heroism; but afterwards there is a change. He looks so bedraggled, so wild in his eyes, so weird in his comic exhaustion, that his friends respond as to a spent ferocity one must respect. After three baths, he slowly begins to return to awareness; but it is awareness now of a different self. The initiation, however silly, however shy of the dignity of ancient tribal initiation, has worked its magic: "The wine of conquest was gone out of him, but in the cool emptiness remained a nuclear conviction" (105). Henceforth, he is Tim. The circumstances are still those of the play-like world of high school, and maturation is a long way off; but, in the cold fury of his selfless struggle, he has felt an American schoolboy's version of the nuclear, a sense of the generative primordial; and he will never again be quite the same schoolboy.

Sacred growth in America, of course, cannot suggest a straight line of progression, ever-upwards, on a neat chart. There are moments of success, moments of defeat, wanderings in a land antagonistic to the uncommercialized and unrational nature of rites of passage. Yet gradually Tim is being converted to the nuclear. On one occasion, he feels himself in a "league of dumb adoration of being" (106); another time he feels a "sympathetic ascension" (107) with trembling leaves. It is as if he were "hunting himself" (108), a self "nearly forgotten" in the "leaves of the magic wilderness within him" (107). What he is feeling is "the birth of the world," the power of the original creation, the source of all energy (108). He is learning the sacredness of all existence.

Still, one must go to school, and to parties where youngsters—
giggling at their own comic and impertinent blossoming toward
adulthood—play games called "spin the bottle" and "post office."
Tim, in gaunt pain, makes a fool of himself. "It would be many
years yet," Clark writes, "before he lost the saintly or foolish
conviction that the world was what he felt it to be" (133). He
has felt the hand of archetypal authority—a hand many of us
feel only when we go gaping into death—but he still manages
to avoid what "would have been his first sharp lesson in realism"
(174–75). He bumbles his way through a kissing game, fails to
realize that Rachel Wells would not want to be the tennis partner
of a sophomore Tristram who worships her in pain and ecstasy,
and does not realize that the "St. Francis order of his room"
(180) is only a "token, a promise" (180) of unity. He has learned
that, with luck, he can "run with the stallion," just as he has, at
times, felt "the deep, sad kinship of everything" (108), just as
he has had moments of pure unity with wordless prayers or with
music; but he is still, in personality if not in character, a romantic.

It is only much later, well into manhood, that he comes close
to a realistic understanding of unity. A long lyrical passage on the
nuclear, actually from the viewpoint of Tim the adult, marks the
beginning of the third section of Book I; appropriately so, I feel,
for the beginning of a new stage in Tim's growth occurs when he
realizes that his "instead-of talk" (199), his obsessive monologues
on sports, represents a failure to shape nuclear energies in a
realistic way. For the first time, Tim begins to develop a sense
of humor (200), a hint at least of the ironically American sense
of sacrality which marks his later development. Book I, in short,
is a lyrical and ironic record of Tim's wavering progress from a
child's sense of the sacred toward a realistic sense of the sacred,
from abstract images of himself and the world through a more
concrete image of himself in an abstract world, and toward a
realistic image of himself as an ironically comic yet holy member
of a realistic world.

The nuclear, perhaps more than any other single theme, is
central to *The City of Trembling Leaves*. It is sought "by way
of the bone and the flesh" (200), and yet it is a "guiding principle" (200), a knowledge, then, but felt-knowledge, akin to D. H.
Lawrence's blood-knowledge and to Steinbeck's concept of thinking through things. As such, "it can't be trapped in a definition

or pinned on the cork by a formula" (200); for definitions must come humbly before the court of reason, paying homage to its principles rather than to the greater principalities of the archetypal. The nuclear partakes "of the question which remains real while its answers, one by one, are abandoned" (200). It is a movement "toward the God becoming" (200), toward that primal reality which cannot be contained within the small glimmer of men's souls. The "seminal" (200) is part of it, "restraint" is part (201), or the difference between Milton's *Paradise Lost* (which is so finished it has little relevance to the living) and a lyric of Burns (which goes "singing down time" [202]): all of these are part of it. The nuclear, more than anything else, I believe, is Clark's version of the archetypal, the sacred. It is the touch of the original cosmos, a profound glimpse but never the possessive attainment; and it is for Clark the central principle of art, religion, and life.

VI   *Rites of Passage in Reno, Nevada*

For Tim Hazard, the vision is as yet only a flicker. The closing parts of Book I are an instance of the "downward path to wisdom." Tim still falls into "instead-of talk" (see 233 ff.), still flees into fantasy (see the end of Chapter 26); and the final chapter, "The Fall of the House of Hazard," is purposefully a reference to the Poe story. The House of Hazard, while not doomed with the horror of the House of Usher, while gifted with certain sad beauties, has crumbled from within itself. Yet there has been a movement toward ironic perspective; Tim is prepared for the next rite of passage through the streets of his American life.

In Book II, the irony becomes more pronounced, partially because childhood merits only gentle irony, but mainly because Tim is now more conscious of the ironic conditions of his pilgrimage. In the "dark library of the interior" (340), exact transition points cannot be fixed; but Tim has entered a troubled age, the aftermath that follows the shocks of initiation. Clark, whose lyrical abilities have not been given their deserved praise, describes this stage of his hero's development as "the terrible adolescence of the mind, which follows that of the body, the time during which reality gradually emerges streaming from the sea of dreams, but in a primal chaos, an awful birthday of the world"

(341). Tim, that is, now admits objective reality into his consciousness; but Clark's story is not the typical story of illusion and reality. The "birthday" is not shocking because of socio-economic realities; the shock is that reality comes in "primal chaos," with old and terrible force. The need is not to adjust to a peer group or to economic impositions; the need is to shape primal reality, the power of the nuclear, into contemporary shapes in Reno, Nevada, in the twentieth century. It is for this reason that Clark's sacrality is ironic. He admits into his vision a primal reality he has had the courage to feel, and yet he keeps to the historical pressures of his own time and admits also the ego, the mind, the necessity of moral responsibility.

However bold this stroke, it amounts to the opening of a modern Pandora's Box; for it is man's conscious reasoning, his assumption of high moral responsibilities, the democratic individual's insistence on understanding the real, which has numbed his sensibilities to the touch and voice of the archetypal. There is a supreme irony, then, in the emergence within Tim of the academic: "He'd tell himself that if he ever wrote serious music it would be just that, serious, studious, correct stuff, the music of a scholar" (346). As he begins to read more rational books, as he becomes more "maturely" concerned with his career as a composer, Tim develops an edge of bitterness to his irony (351, 372). He becomes too rationally conscious to create. "A falseness creeps in," he writes in a letter, "I float to the surface [the rational mind, the empirical observer] and labor like a scholar" (419). At times the problem is so acute he turns to self-mockery, making bitterly sportive musical jokes against himself.

In "The Mountain," however, as suggested by the uncharacteristic brevity and straightforwardness of the title, the irony is of a different type. This is an especially important chapter, the one in which Rachel and Tim make a ritual mountain climb. Both are grown now, and the adolescent desperation of Tim's ardor has mellowed. The relation is gentle, the teasing about Tim's ritual is respectful, and the uncomplicated events of the experience are told with quiet power. Tim initiates Rachel, telling her about the guardians, about the necessity of waiting to see if you are accepted. They touch water. They feel the pull of mountain. A sense of unity develops. Rachel teases Tim into taking his ritual naked swim, and she joins him. At first, he will not look at her;

later, it becomes possible to look without despoiling anything. There follows the warmth of the campfire and then the easing out of a sacred experience in the long hike back down the mountain. For Edmund Wilson, the scene is a disappointment. Tim, Wilson complains, "is too shy to make love to her," and the relationship between them trails off.[9]

What Wilson has missed, it seems to me, is an instance of irony founded in paradox.[10] There is a deliberate tension between the bemused yet serious and even religious tone of the scene and the chapter which follows. The sense of unity which both feel is not, within the scene itself, subjected to any contrary tones other than a mild teasing which in no way undercuts the "mark of the eternal" (403) which both feel they have witnessed. The following chapter title, however, returns to the satiric tone typical of the novel: "About Certain Signs of Altitude Hangover, and the Accidental Reunion of the Houses of Hazard and Turner" (405). The last line of "The Mountain"—"It seemed to Tim that they were very much together"—provides a subtle transition: it *seemed* to Tim. The genuineness of his solemn agreement with Rachel's admonitions about job hunting, however, is given short shrift in the opening sentence of the next chapter: "Tim didn't go out at once and find the job that was to save him" (405). The tension that Clark has constructed is a tension between the sacrality of the mountain climb and the sacrality of the workaday world. The unity which Tim thought he felt was not an illusion. The archetypal reality does exist. The awesome burden of Tim's pilgrimage in life, however, is to shape that unity into his practical life. For his pilgrimage, there is the respect of a straightforward style. For his efforts in practicality, there is the chiding of an ironic style. He dreamed in pain of a mystic unity with Rachel, now he has been rewarded, the reward is real, and yet nothing has changed. Tim Hazard does not yet have sacred wholeness; he has not yet learned to live with his mind.

VII *Henry Adams and Domestic Sacrality*

The section on Henry Adams, in Chapter 37, provides an interesting insight into the nature of Tim's plaguing intellectualism. The reason for Tim's affinity with Adams is clear: the image of the Virgin—symbolic of a felt unity destroyed by the disunity of

the dynamo, the monster machine created out of the conscious
mind's devotion to science—would have an obvious appeal to a
man whose life is a sacred pilgrimage in a modern world. It is
Tim's objections to Adams that are revealing. His objections, ap-
pearing in the form of a letter, are that the Virgin was, actually,
"that highly unvirginal Blanche of Castile" (426) and that Adams
was "a mite arbitrary in nominating the Virgin" (426). Granting
that Adams praises the "anonymous masons, architects, and glass-
makers," Tim asks pointedly, "why are they anonymous?" (426).
The ground rules for this examination are typical of democracy.
The selection of the Queen is suspect, and the supposed unity,
the heterogeneous society, snobbishly reduces the artisan to an
undemocratic anonymity. Adams' real concern is not, after all,
with the people. Significantly, Tim turns again to Lincoln, the
primal hero of democracy; and again Lincoln is called "nuclear"
(427). Tim's efforts toward sacrality must include democratic
responsibilities. Adams, he feels, was "in love with a stained-glass
Virgin" (428). Tim himself, ironically, has made of Rachel a
stained-glass virgin, has fallen victim once more to the dream of
perfection which lures the sacred man toward the most destructive
type of imperfection; yet in his analysis of Adams he shows promise.

Tim's struggles toward realism, in fact, distinguish him from
Lawrence Black, whose story, Clark explains, is much like Tim's.
The chief difference is that Black cannot overcome his love of the
perfect. Black's "own enormous conscience" (435), the mark of
his native tendency to be too analytical and too aware of self,
drives him into an obsessive sense of guilt about money, the
practical world, even those who love him; and this obsession
poisons finally his talent for art.

The pattern of Tim's growth, this part told as it were by refrac-
tion, continues in the madly comic section on Knute Fenderson.
Here the love of perfection has become so fanatic, so unrealistic,
that Clark moves into farce. The culmination of this episode in
Tim's life occurs not so much with Teddy Quest, the too-neat
technician, or with Tim's quick-changes from one kind of music
to another, or even with his love of Eileen O'Connor, as it does
in Stephen Granger's mock-heroic and farcical biography of
Knute Fenderson. Fenderson's actual fanaticism for purity and
perfection are exaggerated by Granger, but the truth of the exag-

geration is biting. It is a farcical version of what is told seriously
in the story of Lawrence Black and of what very nearly ruins
Tim himself.

Tim's salvation, his arriving at questions which are themselves
better than answers, comes in humble ways. Clark's sacred man,
without surrendering his fundamental dedication to primal reality,
is domesticated. The primal reality can become a realistic force,
Tim learns, partially through a paradoxical view of time, partially
through learning that life is a process of becoming, a state of
being one achieves—at least for the moment—and not in some
ecstasy of magic answers.

On the story level, Tim comes to feel that it is Mary, his childhood sweetheart, who is real, with whom he is truly in love. He
comes to see that Helen, despite her hardness, is right to say that
Lawrence Black is "in love with failure" (591), that what has
ruined him is "a destructive desire for perfection" (610). He finds
meaning in a simple statement of love for Mary, in a long search
for the lost and wandering Lawrence Black, in playing folk music
for people who have helped him. The tone moves, again appropriately I think, into something reminiscent of *The Grapes of
Wrath*—a tone of affection which runs the risk of sentimentality.

None of this, however, is to suggest that the novel ends with
a pat message or that it returns to the easy folk-affirmations of
the front-porch swing. After so many failures, Tim finally begins
to compose his "Symphony of the Trembling Leaves," "and this
time it came" (685). The important word is "came." The symphony is not a product of conscious or intellectual effort, nor of
mystical inspiration. It *comes* because Tim, without achieving
any perfection, has betrayed neither the primal nor the realistic.
His state of being is presented emblematically by the closing
scene: he is watering his lawn, his children are at play, and there
is music in the house. The trembling leaves have not been explained, and there is no guarantee for tomorrow, no suggestion
that Tim became a great composer and lived happily ever after;
but some shape, at least for this time, has been given to primal
reality, a shape which is realistic to life in the moribund city,
beneath the shadow of the indifferent mountain.

The novel, it seems to me, may depend too much on a lyrical
quality, too much on a musical composition the reader cannot
hear. The ending might have been based more in the chief narra-

tive line, perhaps in a moral choice involving Mary and Lawrence rather than in a realization of values which were, more or less, waiting for him. The wisdom of using Walt Clark as a narrator is also puzzling, at least to me. Certainly, the efforts to explain how Clark the narrator could have such intimate knowledge of Tim Hazard are a disturbance. Other faults could be found. Helen never quite succeeds as a character, and some of the devices—Teddy Quest's mystic gesture for example—are not successful. The novel as a whole, however, is in my judgment a successful attempt to achieve a daring combination of the primordial and the modern. Clark gives us, I think, both the awesomeness of original energies and the pathos of the domestic. The American schoolboy and the sacred mountain both are real.

CHAPTER 5

A Personal and Malignant Doom:
The Track of the Cat

THE man of reason believes that dreams are a distortion of logic and practicality, a rationalization of everyday experience the conscious mind is reluctant to face. The man of sacrality believes that dreams represent a discovery of reality, an unconscious revelation of truths the conscious mind is unable to produce. As in the oft-noted distinction between Freud and Jung, the difference is between the unconscious as a repository of repressions from the conscious mind and the unconscious as a repository of archetypal meanings. The difference—and this too has been remarked frequently—should not be exaggerated. According to both views, the conscious mind (at least for modern man) has a tendency to reject the experience of the unconscious; and, according to both views, the unconscious experience (brought into the conscious mind most often by dreams) has symbolic and usually mythic content.

Perhaps the central difference can best be seen in terms of the desired response: what should a man *do* about the workings of his unconscious? For Freud and the rationalists, experience repressed into the unconscious, when not purged by conscious analysis, may lead to a distortion of everyday life. One may lose contact with reality and become psychotic. Reason must not hide behind dreams. Reason must unravel the mystery of dream symbolism and thus—in cases of mental illness—restore the individual to healthy realism. For Jung and the tradition of sacrality, however, the translation of unconscious experience into rational meaning may distort the true and archetypal meaning of unconscious experience. Dreams are not repressions *from* the conscious mind so much as personalized versions of archetypal meanings which can be observed empirically by reason but which are different from reason in kind and superior to reason in quality.[1]

I *The Journey Within the Unconscious*

Walter Clark's *The Track of the Cat*—perhaps the finest Western novel written—must be granted its own integrity apart from all comparisons and possible sources; but readers who assume a Freudian or a practicalist definition of dreams and reality will misunderstand the symbolism of the black painter, and they will be unable to see the structural connection between the story of the hunt and the story of the family. The cat which is hunted by Curt Bridges is an actual beast; it has killed and mutilated cattle and it kills Curt's brother Arthur. But the cat which chases Curt, which sends him fleeing in panic toward a cliff, is an imagined cat, a projection of his own unconscious. Curt had felt that the imagined cat—the supposedly black painter of myth and magic—represented a distortion of everyday reality. What he begins to see, too late, is that it is his own factualist definition of himself which represents a distortion of everyday reality.

I am again suggesting that we need to understand better the relevant context of Walter Clark's novels. In a general way, the context of *The Track of the Cat* is obvious. Curt's hunt is a mythologem of the journey into the unconscious. Standard works on ancient mythology describe the general implications of his journey. Joseph Campbell's description of the "tyrant-monster," for example, seems an apt description of Curt: "Self-terrorized, fear-haunted, alert at every hand to meet and battle back the anticipated aggressions of his environment, which are primarily the reflections of the uncontrollable impulses to acquisition within himself, the giant of self-achieved independence is the world's messenger of disaster, even though, in his mind, he may entertain himself with humane intentions."[2]

Each detail of this description applies to Curt. Further, with only slight variants, Campbell's description of the "standard path of the mythological adventure of the hero" applies in detail to Hal, the youngest of the Bridges brothers: "A hero ventures forth from the world of common day into a region of supernatural wonder: fabulous forces are there encountered and a decisive victory is won: the hero comes back from this mysterious adventure with the power to bestow boons on his fellow man." [3]

Or one could turn to any of a number of standard sources and find numerous mythological parallels: the accident, the breaking of a taboo which unleashes the annual appearance of evil, in this case, Art's failure to make the icon in time for the unseasonable snows;[4] the annual appearance of evil in the form of a beast;[5] the father who is like the "carnival king";[6] Curt's disorientation in time and space; Joe Sam's need to suffer;[7] the death of animals and deviation from the norm.[8] Such specifics, furthermore, have the expected mythological quality. The comparisons are not merely fortuitous. Clark's psychology, in fact, is directly comparable to primitive psychology. His heroes do not mature against their father or against their Heavenly Father; they mature against the cosmic father. Their Oedipal complex is primordial, not filial. They must attain that separation from the mundane which is a discovery of one's identity in the mundane.

Study of these themes in *The Track of the Cat* could profitably be expanded at length, but my point is that such comparisons must be made in the light of Clark's original and Americanized handling of mythological materials. *The Track of the Cat* is about the frontier, the rape of the land for commercial purposes (the father moans the loss of the golden days of San Francisco; Curt wants to get his stake and get out to civilization); the Hawthornesque theme of ancestral guilt (the disinheriting of the Indian); and—perhaps most typical of all—the initiation of a lad into manhood.[9] And the characters too are in a general way typically American: the father who drinks too much, who dreamed of getting rich quick, whose talking bitterness is that of thousands of American fathers after the dream is over; the mother, who is a martyr to housework, a narrowly self-righteous Protestant who nags grown sons, is prudish, who sits in harsh judgment on all her knotted world; the go-getter son, Curt, who wants to make money and get to the big city and who is always just barely on this the human side of brutality; the dreaming son, Arthur, who is "different," who reads too much, is sensitive, kind, and strangely prophetic but ineffectual, the saint-victim; the youngest son, Hal, for whom there is hope, provided he meets the great trial that awaits him near the end of the novel; the psychological cripple, Grace, the unmarried and unmarriageable sister, incapacitated by the barren atmosphere of the family; the somewhat idealized good American girl, Gwen, warm yet moral, patient yet strong, who is from the wrong side of the tracks, loved by the young hero and the object of older lusts; and the old man of a minority race, Joe Sam, the Indian who, like Faulkner's Sam Fathers, instructs the young hero from a distance, guides his journey into a world that once was the domain of minority man.

These familiar characters, of course, have their counterparts in mythology; but the question is, why have most of Clark's critics failed to see the connection between the mythical hunt and the domestic barrenness? The answer, I believe, is that mythology is thought to be something which happens to someone else. It may be real in ancient India or on a South Sea island, perhaps on a symbolic hunt in undomesticated mountains; but a myth cannot survive on a bustling American sidewalk, cannot withstand the scientific investigation of modern psychology or sociology, and therefore cannot be relevant to an American family consisting of recognizable and realistic American characters. We take mythology only in a negative way, only when its loss results in a barrenness we are all too familiar with to call unrealistic.

Clark's broad subject, after all, is comparable to the subject which has dominated twentieth-century literature: the loss of a center, the loss of an emotionally meaningful contact with our sources. And these are the themes with which modern man is so familiar: the continued measuring of all things before the standards of prestige and practicality; the enslavement to the intellect which results, finally, in an inability to love; the loss of one's capacity to feel. This is what has happened to Edward Albee's Young Man in *The American Dream*; to Eliot's Gerontion; and, in a different way, to many of Faulkner's dehumanized victims and villains of the Mississippi wasteland. Such characterizations are also familiar to readers through the offices of cultural studies (*The Lonely Crowd, The Organization Man*); and, since they can be gotten at in terms of statistics and current events and with at least the tone of a scientific method, we can respond and say "Yes, this is real." Our sensibilities, however, are embarrassed by the writer who feels that if the loss is real, so is the presence. For Walter Clark, Gerontion would not be in a wasteland if the black painter were merely a dream, merely the distorted repression of a sick consciousness unable to face reality.

If primordial energies are terrifyingly present on our streets today, is it not perhaps a mistake to say that primordial meanings
are quaintly irrelevant? If facts and reason constitute the only
real knowledge, why are we so nervous?

II *Homunculus and the Facts: Practicality Redefined*

Much of Clark's work—most specifically *The Track of the Cat*
—is an implicit prediction of the animalistic and apparently un-
motivated violence which has been so disturbing to Americans
in the 1960's. Our understanding of realism, Clark has warned, is
dangerously one-dimensional. The specific dramatization of the
warning is in the character of Curt Bridges, who confidently
fancies himself a man of hard-nosed practicality. Curt takes
tough-guy pride in ridiculing dreams before the standards of
one-dimensional realism. Arthur, Curt proclaims, cannot "ranch"
his dreams, that is, man cannot live on shadows but must live on
food, something of physical substance; and this necessity is supposed to reveal the foolishness of men who talk of insubstantial
realities. The cat which is killing their cattle, Curt insists, is a
physical cat; and it can be killed with a regulation bullet. It
needs no magic. It is no spook, no black and mystic painter.

Curt's counterparts today among the American citizenry believe much the same thing: that which is wrong in the land
cannot be set right by the nonsense of dreams. Yet this same
realist lives in a house without joy; is trying to convince himself
that he does not have an ulcer; blames his son's insolence and
wildness on bad associates (or calls bad behavior a "mistake,"
the current euphemism for "sin"); and persists, stubbornly, in
believing that what troubles the land is some version of the
physical cat, something that comes within the sanctions of reason
and practicality. Walter Clark knows well the powers of the
physical cat, but he writes of a much more powerful beast which
cannot be killed with bullets, any more than a cultural violence
that is born of barrenness can be cured with love expressed
through the gift of an automobile or with the hiring of psychol-
ogist-priests as parental substitutes. Clark writes of the deeper
realism of a "personal and malignant doom" [10] which comes to
those who fail to recognize the archetypal realities of the human
experience. It is the doom of those who mock their own homuncu-

lus, and get away with it until the day of crisis, when archetypal energies, distorted by denial, break from the inner self in undirected violence.

It follows, I think, that the two most common critical comments on *The Track of the Cat* are inaccurate: the cat only seems to be a Western version of Moby Dick, and the young Hal only seems to represent a combination of Curt's practicality and Arthur's spirituality. Moby Dick and the cat are comparable in that both represent a device into which characters read their own psychological predilections, but Ahab is killed by an actual whale. When Curt runs from the cat to his death, there is no cat at all.

Curt's practicality and Arthur's spirituality could be combined only in a world run on linear time. Clark's point is that Curt is fatally impractical. The archetypal meaning of Curt's experience is not separate from everyday life; rather, archetypal meaning is present in everyday life in eminently practical ways. A common sense which drives one to run screaming, pitching headlong into death, running from no physical threat, is after all a very poor version of common sense. It is even inaccurate to say that Arthur fails on practical grounds while succeeding on spiritual grounds. Arthur's failure is that he has lost the ability to "come and go" (7) between the two worlds, has lost, that is, the sacred unity of the two worlds which is the mark of spiritual success in Clark's fictive world. Though he is sincere and admirably kind, Arthur is the older brother; and he has let Curt assume command. He checks but does not stop the pecking order which Curt has established, and that order is part of the evil which Hal, in the end, has a chance to correct. Only the reader who assumes a Puritan split between this world and the next will be content to say that Arthur can represent the attainment of the spiritual and yet be out of touch with practical life. The spiritual hero in linear time may find the soul and the body in inalienable conflict, but the spiritual hero in cyclical time earns his heroism by his attainment of harmony, by his discovery of God in hand, not God in an abstract Heaven.

In the context of this cyclical concept of unity, the structure of the novel, specifically the relation of the hunting scene to the domestic scenes, is clear. Grace's tirade against the family may serve to represent the domestic scene: "I've need to say this. We all need to. Even the house needs to. It's rotten with lies and greed and bad dreams. Arthur knew; oh, how he knew. But he was too kind-hearted. He always forgave everything. All he'd do was make little jokes that told the truth if you listened to them. But you [the mother] and your God don't hear little jokes. And Curt and Father don't even have a God, not any kind. Only money. Only self-importance and wanting their own way, and money, money, money" (173).

Curt's tracks lead back to the house. It is there, in his failure of being and not in any single act of bad will, that the source of Curt's malignancy is to be found. And though the parents' circumstances are different from those of Curt when he becomes lost in the snow, their lack of orientation in the universe is just as fatal. What drives Curt to his death has chased them into a domestic type of the same death and, with a proper crisis, would unleash their beast. A caged and betrayed homunculus in the home is a nag, a thing of ploys and pecking; in the mountains, in a snowstorm, he can kill.

The personalities differ, importantly; but the one-dimensional barrenness of their lives is much the same for the father, the mother, and Curt. Early in the novel, when Arthur and Hal contemplate the possibility of using the capacities of the ranch to help Hal establish his own family, the mother mocks their plans: "It's practical facts I'm tryin' to get straight . . . , not dreams" (27). And a little later, when Hal explains the Indians' belief in the magic of names, the father denounces such stuff as "pure, romantic rubbish"; and then, in a way that suggests a legion of fictive and actual American fathers, he swings to an attack on Arthur's reading: "Novels and poetry and fairy stories about the ancient Greeks and the Chinese and the Lord only knows what. Not a dependable fact or a piece of usable information in the whole lot. . . . He's as completely a dreamer as Joe Sam himself, only it isn't just by spells" (55).

Despite their vicious separation from one another, father and mother agree in priding themselves on practicality—one hiding behind whiskey, the other behind the Bible—and Curt is quite obviously the favorite of both parents. I do not mean to suggest that their failure is an implicit attack on prudence or an implicit defense of idle dreams. Their failure as parents and as human beings, I am suggesting, is presentational insight into the imprudence of one-dimensional realism, the worshipping of facts in a way that requires the devotee to mock those archetypal yearnings which offer to man a possible unity of himself within himself and of himself within his universe. The father's protestations of culture and the mother's harsh religion cannot provide that unity; for both beliefs are barren, lacking in archetypal energy. Neither belief can provide a means of orientation. The father is not a father at all—but merely a pathetic clown of a father—and the mother has only that sincere and cancerous love which can be generated by the will, by a determined consciousness severed from the vitalizing primordial.

III *The Meeting With Your Self*

The same dangerous devotion to facts and the same contempt for dreams are in Curt, and they prove to be his undoing. After passing Cathedral Rock, the mythical sign of entrance into a foreign space, Curt began to feel as if he were "climbing in a dream on a mountain that wasn't real" (255). The dream persists, and soon he "had no sense at all of the time that was passing, either" (255). He is, like modern man, disoriented in space and time, out of touch with his dark and inner self, alone in the universe with only his pathetically inadequate intellect to guide him among the ancient realities he is now about to meet. Thus Curt, with all his skill in hunting beasts out of the world of facts, is ill-equipped when he comes upon the black painter.

Startled out of the disturbing reverie into which he had fallen, Curt gets set for action; but he experiences a strange loss of confidence:

> The sudden pain of guilt and loss his mind let out into him moved him as if his insides were being twisted, but he didn't know it. He believed the catch in his breath came from excitement, for he was trembling, as he slowly turned the carbine in his hands. The weakness angered him.
>
> God Almighty, he thought, I'm like a kid on his first time out, and forced himself to move slowly and attentively. Even so a tiny dancing remained in his hands and his knees, and there wasn't time to wait it out. (256)

Arthur, Curt had said earlier, cannot "ranch" his dreams; for that which is real is made of substantial stuff. The good is that which you can buy and sell, not dreams; and evil has a tangible cause which a tough man can track down and shoot. But the guilt which now swells twisting up out of Curt's inner self cannot be bought or sold, or shot with bullets made of lead. Nor can the guilt be tracked by the intellect. It is not the guilt of a single act or of conscious intentions. It is guilt of being, the guilt of a man who has been too impractical and too cowardly to regard with awe those archetypal dreams which are the sacred messages of man's connection with the primordial. The "loss" which Curt feels is the loss of that connection, and the failure—far from being a realistic refusal to chase dream-values—is a real impoverishment with deadly consequences.

Curt, at this point, still looks for the reasonable explanation: he is excited, he tells himself, his brother is recently dead, he is over-reacting to a stimulus. The excitement, however, is much deeper. His thought that he is "like a kid on his first time out" is but one of dozens of instances of a cosmic irony. Curt makes the statement in search of something far from the truth. He is in fact very experienced, very capable, and he has been out hundreds of times; it is thus absurd, he thinks, to act in a way so opposite from his expectations. But ironically he is a "kid on his first time out." This is the first time in his thirty-seven years that he has met the cat that cannot be killed with bullets, the cat, that is, which makes him confront himself.[11]

Shortly after, Curt "believes" he sees the cat (280), protests that he is "in undirected flight himself" (281), loses all sense of place (283), struggles manfully to keep the "compass of his reasoning" in line with the "compass of his body" (283), and surrenders finally "the last pretense of keeping up the hunt" (283). His factualist intellect cannot deal with the primordial realities that guilt and crises have unleashed from within. He is now the hunted; and, though he does not realize it, he is also, in the sense that personal energies have distorted themselves into projections of the black painter, the hunter. Pathetically, he persists in thinking his reason can save him. Desperately, he repeats "his formula for salvation" (310), mechanical directions for getting back home; but there is no formula for salvation. Factualist reason cannot guide man in the sacred mountains of the universe.[12] Factualist reason, however, is all that Curt has, and so he turns to a frantic mathematics:

Say I can see seventy-five yards, he thought. I'd guess it's more than that, but say seventy-five to stay on the safe side. It would take, say, five seconds for him to cover that much in this snow. It takes me, say, he thought, counting the steps he took and judging their rate, five seconds to take five steps. I'm giving myself margin on both those counts too.

"Take a look around you every five steps," he concluded aloud, "and he can't catch you napping." (315)

But his math, as Curt soon realizes, is wrong. The "dark, internal traitor of time" (333), primordial time, is gaining "power over him steadily" (333); and that night, trying to stay awake and keep clock time by cigarettes, he fails, after four attempts, in a simple problem in multiplication (358). In one of his moments of elation, Curt is like "the scientist who has reduced disorderly nature to a quotable mathematical certainty" (359). But man's little schoolboy intellect, as Curt is reluctantly coming to realize, cannot chart primordial reality. Like Buck in *The Watchful Gods*, Curt hears from the "internal monitor," a voice out of the conscious which warns against arrogance. Repeatedly, in both works, the warning is heard when the reason begins to deal too confidently with reality. With Curt, this last and feeble touch with reality collapses: "The monitor abdicated with a long, internal wail, and he dropped the useless carbine and turned to run" (364). He is running to his death.[13]

IV *The Profane House*

Curt Bridges does not panic because Clark took him into a region symbolic of ancient but now dead mythology. Curt panics because of what is going on now in thousands of homes all across this land. The wasteland theme, the images of discontent, the theme of lost identity, the theme of loss of values, the search for something to belong to: the concepts which have characterized twentieth-century literature are what Clark thinks of as the theme of disorientation. Modern man has lost the ability to hear the authoritative voice of the archetypal, has thereby distorted archetypal energies away from a possible connection with affirmative values, and now finds himself on the edge of panic without knowing why.

Curt's panic, as I have suggested, is caused by the barrenness

of his domestic life, a divisive and destructive policy of narrow-
ness which is supported chiefly by the father, the mother, by Curt
himself, and which has incapacitated Grace and wounded Arthur.
Symbolic and structural elements relating the hunting scene to
the domestic scene are sufficient in number and in richness to
call for dozens of studies, not for a single chapter. Certainly, full-
length articles need to be written on ghost imagery, the recurrent and always ironic jokes, the technique of psychological
irony, the theme of memory, patterns of color imagery, the image of shadows, the theme of tracking, bird symbolism, and
mythic transformations. These topics and others, furthermore, are
worked out elaborately and carefully; and all help to make the
connection between sterility in the home and panic on the mountain. Here I can only hope to suggest the connection.

Curt has several motives to drive him on the hunt. His economic interests are at stake, he wants sincerely to revenge his
brother's death, his male ego is on the line; but of at least equal
importance is his desire to "show" Gwen, the little "Welchy."
She has not been defeated by his hot-eyed and mocking flirta-
tions; rather, she seems to have bested him or—even worse—not
to have considered him very important. He is furious, and he
vows repeatedly to "show her," to get the black pelt for her, and
to make her pay for it. This is a degraded version of an ancient
rite, the winning of the maiden by conquest or by a gift which
results from a conquest. In general, it is an emotion all men feel,
the offering of some accomplishment as a means of wooing one's
sweetheart. The courtship in Curt's version is entirely destructive. There is no indication that he is in any sense a rival of
Hal's; he fancies himself the superior brother, of course, the irre-
sistible male; but his half-serious, half-joking idea is contemptu-
ous: he can bed the little wench if he chooses to, and Hal can
have what's left over.

The father, the mother, and Curt all call Gwen a whore. The
father calls his own wife a whore; and Hal, though he does not
say it aloud, thinks of calling the mother by the same name. The
father also accuses Gwen of being the cause of Curt's death, and
Curt accuses Art of wanting to play the "loving priest" (69).
The mother, quite simply, is a whore in the sense that she allowed her legal husband to sleep with her without giving him
love and in exchange for her share of all the goods he would

ever after acquire. She sold her body for value received and, according to the father, got very much the better end of the deal (177–78). In Gwen's case, the accusations are caused superficially by class prejudice (there is no evidence against her, as Curt admits to himself); but the deeper cause is a lesson in original sex, and it is the same failure which has ruined the mother as a woman.

Gwen, in mythical terms, is the anima, the soul as female, the bewitching figure who is at once love and danger.[14] But Clark's mythology is always his own, always a modern and Americanized version which is more a creation than a redaction. Gwen troubles the mother and arouses hatred because she has the pure and natural charm the mother has sacrificed on the altar of Momism. Curt is resentful because she will not bow to his role as the King of Practical Action—and it hurts because his power has never before been matched. She is in touch with original femaleness, untainted by self-righteousness or by lust; and her presence, her feminine being, is thus disruptive to those whose values are severed from all connections with the original.

Hal, after watching Gwen's warm and active goodness in a time of stress, analyzes his fiancée accurately:

> Curt'd call her a priestess now, he thought. Or medicine woman [as Curt had mockingly, not realizing he spoke the truth, called Arthur a medicine man]. And she is, too, he thought. She wants what Arthur wanted. She couldn't say it in words, the way he could, maybe, but it's the same thing. She doesn't like the God that's in there with Mother now any more than he did. It's a God for the dead. Dad was right about that much, anyway.
>
> And hers is for life, he thought, looking down at the blue hood. It's the God of Life against the God of Death. . . . (130)

The God of Death is served by the mother's self-righteous materialism and by that immoral fear which makes her curse the honest passion she sees in Gwen and hide whatever passion she may once have felt within herself. Such a God does not represent a universe which includes the evil energies of the black painter and the indifference of mountain spaces and the beauty of simple ceremony, and such a God does not represent the harshness that is in all men (even Hal feels it rise up from inside) or the capacity for love so fundamental that it is felt—too late—by the

mother, by Curt, and—with a dulled alcoholic touch—by the
father. Such a deity is a God of Death because He is man's
mental and unrealistic concoction: to serve such values is to
serve an illusion. The God of Life, on the contrary, includes the
ugly along with the beautiful, evil along with good. This is
Gwen's God, as we see in her tolerance, her unabashed and
guiltless passion for Hal, her understanding of the father's sad
vestige of the party-spirit and the mother's destructive sermon-
izing. Unlike Arthur, Gwen is not in touch with the machinery
of Oriental thought. There is no evidence that she is a reader or
a deep thinker. She has learned, apparently, from living and
from a continuity of good will, from a willingness to accept the
primordial lesson that God must be made of all the disparate
elements we see in life; and she has her soul in better balance
than anyone else in the novel. It is not her class or her actions,
then, that cause resentment. It is her being.

The father, who may once have been capable of seeing the
quality of Gwen, is now too deeply mired in the psychological
graves of his own consciousness. He cannot remember who
Gwen is (150), and he keeps calling her Curt's intended (176,
179, 180). Similarly, the mother struggles to remember how
Arthur was earlier, or what happened to some value long since
lost. Arthur, Curt, and Hal also struggle to remember something,
some haunting and vague yet naggingly important experience
out of the past which seems, strangely, to predict the future.
Herein, I think, in ways that are at once mythical and realistically contemporary, is the most significant of the methods by
which Clark unifies his novel.

The specifics of this method could be analyzed at length; few
novels, I think, are so carefully structured. The dreams, to sketch
briefly a few items in one technique of the novel, are both mythical and realistically contemporary in content; and they invoke
profound insights into the past of man, that of the Bridges men
specifically; and they predict a future that is determined by the
conditions and actions of the past. Classical mythology is filled
with different types of strange warnings; and the sense of such
warnings, for modern man at least, is that knowledge of present
or past flaws in being may, for an acute observer, foretell the
future. Joe Sam is able to foretell Curt's future not because he
has magical powers but because he knows from experience the

fate of those too egoistic to heed their "inner monitor," too arrogant to respect the primordial energies of nature or to realize that a man's homunculus is never completely tamed, never completely house-broken.

Crime and punishment in an archetypal universe, to put it simply, require a narrative context. Both sin and virtue are always in progress; no event exists in isolation. Events are important, necessarily so, but being is always more important. Clock time is subsumed under cyclical time. This accounts for the characteristic concern of Western writers with what may strike an Eastern ear as irrelevant detail (the recurrent invocation of and references to nature, for example, even while describing a dramatic event), and it accounts for the recurrent warnings in *The Track of the Cat.*

Warnings occur in Arthur's dream at the opening of the novel (5), in Hal's first dream (135), in Curt's first dream (269), and in Curt's two dreams just before his death (353, 362); and these are but a few of the foreboding hints that fill the novel. The ones listed, furthermore, are strikingly similar: all involve the danger of a loved one who is perhaps a brother, perhaps one's self; the danger is always vague and changing; and there is always a struggle to remember or a frustrated effort to give warning. Clark's patterns of this type are amazingly explicit and extensive: the bare left hand (4, 71, 94, 396), hearing the voice of someone known and loved (3, 135, 235), the dreamer who seems in familiar territory yet does not know where he is (4, 269, 278), the association of the cat and some nearby willows (57, 68, 135, 270). On the story level, all three brothers admonish themselves to stay alert while tracking, and all three debate within themselves. Joe Sam's wife had her neck broken by the black painter of long ago; the steer apparently broke "its own neck . . . running blind, and in the dark" (72); Arthur's neck is broken (95–97); Joe Sam breaks the quail's neck (158); and Curt, running blind and in the dark, fell onto rock, head first, almost certainly breaking his own neck.

These patterns, obviously, are not confined to certain types of sensibility; they move within all three brothers, and they include past, present, and future, and both man and animal. They include, also, recurrent patterns of imagery. Arthur, in the opening dream, finds himself in a mountain that is familiar and yet strange. He cannot remember having seen it before. It seems "to him to belong somewhere as far away as the Andes or the Himalayas or the moon" (5). Immediately before his panicked race to death, Curt realizes that he is lost, that he is in mountains irrevocably foreign: "He was in entirely strange mountains; they might as well have been the Andes or the Himalayas or the mountains of the moon" (365).

That Joe Sam is not merely living in a dream is shown by his ability to read such patterns. What he sees in the future, that is, has tracks which extend far into the past. The poverty of being which leads to Curt's death is not new. What Joe Sam knows is that the domestic pecking order of the ranch which feeds Curt's illusions will provide no protection from the dormant beast within Curt himself, will be no protection when impersonal nature and personal guilt reveal the hollowness beneath the proud breast. This is not to suggest, however, that Joe Sam's foreknowledge is a product of reasoning about symbolism. The meanings of the unconscious are mythical rather than symbolical. The bare hand, for example, suggests nakedness, a covert need to return to a betrayed and unconscious self; but it suggests also a non-logical kinship among ironic victims. The dream territory which is both familiar and strange represents, more simply, the unconscious itself. Arthur and Curt have been there, as have all men; but even Arthur has become so involved in the commercialization of the land and in the wars of the isolated ego that the land of the true self now seems as strange as the most exotic of lands, "as far away as the Andes or the Himalayas or the moon."

V *The Psychology of Tracking*

The patterns of unconscious experience, as Jung has argued, do not require exegesis.[15] They can be interpreted adequately by those who observe honestly the messages which come. The signs of the 1960's were clear enough to Aldous Huxley and George Orwell by the 1940's, and to Matthew Arnold in the 1860's, and the tracks of the cat are clear to the most fact-ridden members of the Bridges family. Even before the death of Arthur, Curt teases his older brother, ostensibly to put the "dreamer" in his place; but his jokes reveal an insight he lacks the courage to accept. Like those he-men Gerald Tetley denounces in *The Ox-*

Bow Incident, Curt is too afraid of "feminine" insight (knowledge which is not hardheaded, practical, factual, provable) to admit its legitimacy.

Still, it is Curt who conjectures that Joe Sam would be "for the cat" (15), who makes mocking jokes about a magic bullet to kill the black painter, and who later realizes but will not admit that his motive in the hunt is as much his desire to appease the frustration he feels before Gwen as it is to revenge Arthur's death or to protect his investment in cattle. Likewise, the mother says that she can "feel" in her "bones" that something is going to happen (30), and her knowledge that the body in Curt's coat is really Arthur's body is evidence that her feelings have an impressive validity. Curt and the mother, then, have heard the archetypal voice at least on occasion, but neither respects that voice until after its warnings have become fact; and Curt is openly blasphemous, turning his insight into rough jokes which predict—and this is the last joke—his own doom.

Those who are mean of spirit lack the capacity to believe what their unconscious tells them. It is difficult even for Arthur, who dreams prophetically of his own death: in both the dream and the actual event the place of death is the same, one hand is bare, the bird image occurs, one hand is raised, and there is a fall. Indeed, the sense of fear, of something wrong in the house, of trouble on the land, is felt by all the characters in the novel. When archetypal realities are betrayed, there is a turbulence in the unconscious. It can shape dreams, send strange tremors of feeling over the skin. The characters and their environment are permeated with warnings, but those who give their allegiance to "usable" facts have too much pride in their reason to admit the reality of a dream; and those who treasure the archetypal but live in an alien time must fight for their very lives.

Tracking, in short, is a difficult task. Americans are born to the bias of cause and effect, and the tendency is to look for an explanation that comes within the realm of reason. All three brothers try to relate tracks to a physical cause; all three look for factualist explanations of dream experience (Arthur dreams that his hand is cold and awakens to find his hand outside the cover, Hal dreams that he hears a shot and later finds that Joe Sam has smashed a bottle, Curt dreams that he is being whipped in the leg but awakens to find that he has burned himself with a cigarette); and all three seem to feel more comfortable when the factualist explanation can be found. The evil that is on the land is a powerful and terrifying thing, and even good men seek the comfort of the tangible explanation, look for something less painful than problems of the soul.

When Hal becomes confused about the activities of Joe Sam, the strange behavior of the crazy old Indian suggests meanings that threaten to destroy the assumptions of the rational mind. Hal stumbles before his own conclusions: "He was briefly possessed by a superstitious notion that everybody on the place was changing toward something strange and evil, but all of them together, and so gradually that no one could see what was happening except when some little hint of the unnatural got out. . . ." (155).

Hal's feeling that his family is "changing toward something strange and evil," of course, is not a "superstitious notion." As a citizen of his times, Hal balks before the awesome challenge, the sacred fact of man's necessary relation with the universe. Modern man is reluctant to absorb the universe, afraid to admit the non-rational and often non-masculine identity of his inner self; and he seeks to mollify his offended modern ego by dismissing his insights as a "superstitious notion." The tracks, nonetheless, are presented to the consciousness: "He'd have to keep his eyes open, be sure of the tracks far enough ahead so they couldn't circle back on him without his knowing it" (156). In this instance, the "he" is Hal; but in other instances the "he" is Arthur, trying to hold the cat's trail until Curt returns to continue the hunt; and Curt, after Arthur's death, reminds himself of dangers only half understood; and, in a more domestic context, Mrs. Bridges belatedly admits that she has not accepted the warnings of danger presented to her eyes.

Negligence in reading tracks, furthermore, is associated with guilt. While pursuing Joe Sam, Hal is suddenly surprised by a profusion of tracks: "The silence came back, and he was ashamed, and a little worried, because he had let them startle him. He should have seen them first, and he certainly should have noticed the spidery writing of their tracks everywhere in the lanes through the brush" (157). While tracking the cat, both Arthur and Curt also become distracted, both also feel guilty for allowing themselves to become distracted; and for all three of the brothers there is an association between literal track and symbolic track, between a duty to track well and a disturbing, vague evocation of something wrong within the home. Each of the brothers has sensed the "personal and malignant doom" that stalks the family, but there is "too much time forgotten between" (157); homunculus has been too long denied, and it has become difficult and even painful to read honestly the signs of an ancient unity which modern man has betrayed. Significantly, it is the home which distracts, for the tracks in the snow—whether those of Joe Sam or the cat—reveal a connection between the inner reality of the Bridges family and the external reality of nature. To protest the reality of dreams symbolizing this connection is to cry in the dark. Man's inner self, however reluctantly, must come before the judgment of archetypal reality.

VI *Sacred Affirmation*

To find his way in the archetypal passages of life (birth, the entrance into adulthood, marriage, the founding of a home, death), man has always needed a mythology.[16] Ceremony is the most common language of mythology, and the Bridges do have ceremony; but theirs are the rites of a hollow and degraded ceremony. The father's manner, for example, is most ceremonial; but it comes in the "same slow, ceremonious defiance" (38) with which he pours his glass one-third full of whiskey and in the way he lights his cigar, "slowly and ceremoniously" (59). It is the ceremony of materialism gone decadent; his dreams are of a San Francisco now dead, but once "the very shrine of wealth and beauty and fashion" (60). Curt, under the strain of Arthur's death, feels a mythic need. Preparing to go after the beast that has killed Arthur, he tries "to think of something to do or say that would make the trifle of ceremony he needed for the parting" (98). He pledges himself to get the cat, even if it takes all winter; but he knows the pledge is inadequate: it "wasn't enough; it didn't fill the bill" (98). "There was," Clark explains, "a long past it didn't make up for . . ." (98). The primordial is more generous than the Christian God in that He is not harsh about tribal prejudice (environmental influence), irrational evil, or body lusts; but He is harsh about salvation. A good will is not enough; the past cannot be washed as clean as snow. The convert must change his being—the flesh as much as the soul—and, for a salvation of being, time is required. Curt, who has lived too long in a false world, does not have enough time.

Joe Sam, though comically and hauntingly ineffectual, does have the sense of ceremony. Even in the simple act of scattering grain for chickens, Joe Sam feels a sense of the sacredness of all life. To watch Sam is, Arthur had once told Hal, "like watching a kind of play" (162). The qualities are those of the haiku: there is "more meaning than you'd think at first." You would have to "hunt for what it meant" (162). Hal's own feelings are much the same, for the simple act strikes him as "a kind of cere-mony" (162). Joe Sam's movements suggest that "the act is holy" (162). The ceremony concludes with a "final rite" (164), and then the "small magic of the ceremony dissolves" (164).

Hal's ability to sympathize with Joe Sam is but one of those qualities which enable him to offer hope for the future. Though not as aggressive as readers might like to see him, he is not yet twenty; and his brothers are thirty-seven and forty. Still, Hal understands and values the mythical predilections of Arthur and Joe Sam, he is kindly and patient with his father, he endures his mother, he is kind to Grace, and he will probably become a strong enough man for Gwen. Through it all, he keeps his head, observes and feels, does his work. And yet he will side with Curt when he thinks it appropriate. His character is not merely one of patient endurance, and neither is he simply a youthful version of common-sense balance. The balance that Hal is developing is the capacity to see the sacred in the everyday. He can sense the holy meanings of a simple act.

Clark's emphasis, I think, is on Hal's growing ability to see the sacred as a presence—a real presence and not a symbolized or intellectualized representation—and yet not separate himself from the mundane, not fall into the sacred doom of ecstasy. Hal's dreams include fabulous beasts, like those on Arthur's elaborate blue blan-ket, a sign of his deep contact with the original world; and yet, un-like Arthur, he wants to marry and have a family and develop a ranch of his own. That his hopes are ordinary ones, perhaps even trite, is precisely the point. The finest type of the modern American dream, Clark seems to feel, is the courage to believe that a practical and passionate domestic life can be, in the most ancient of ways, a holy life.

CHAPTER *6*

Internal Debate as Discipline:
The Watchful Gods

MODERN man is inclined to be arrogant toward anyone who believes in an objective reality outside the domain of reason. If you claim to believe in a reality which is objective, the argument goes, then you imply that I too am obligated to believe; yet you deny the standard of reason, the only standard your audience can use as a check against the pitfalls of subjectivity and bias. How then is one to know if the belief is objective or merely the product of a private whim? What standard does the believer set for himself? Underlying such questions is the assumption that there is no standard other than reason, that reason in some scientific or philosophical form takes in all legitimate approaches to knowledge, that non-reasoned knowledge is bogus. To believe in a reality not in the domain of reason is said to be a mistaken belief in the objectivity of personal opinions.

I make the rather strong claim that this protest against non-reasoned knowledge is arrogant because men of reason have not themselves been able to meet the standard of knowledge they use as a club to hold over men of non-reason. For centuries, European and American philosophers have attempted to find a way to get content into the forms of reason, but they have not succeeded. Students of philosophy know that reason is absolute only in its pure forms, in syllogisms, or in the exercises of Aristotle's magic square. It is easy enough to say that all A is B, all C is A, and to draw a conclusion; but if we change A to "Democrats" or "Catholics" or "Americans," to something which is less than a pure abstraction, then we are hard put to finish even the initial proposition in any way that is not silly. Students of philosophy know also of the tremendous importance of the Cartesian split, of Descartes' reawakening modern man to the realization of the self involved, intrinsically involved, in the effort to relate the concretions of experience to the principles of reason. In my own judgment, the most intellectually noble attempt to put content into reason is that of Immanuel Kant; but, even if Kant did succeed, modern man does not know it; for we find ourselves today in a world in which the most vital philosophies are those of existentialism (which sidesteps the ancient problem by dismissing the universal from court and putting the full burden on man's individual psychology) and scientism (which sidesteps the problem by dismissing both the universal and the individual).

Considering the history of man's efforts to put content into reason, and considering the contemporary status of that effort— a situation so impoverished it has been called the "abdication of philosophy"—it is difficult to understand the general respect for reason except as a cultural habit.[1] Contemporary man, it is true, has become skeptical of reason. He is prone to take pathetic pleasure in exposing the fallibility of human reasoning and to show an even more pathetic deference to the non-emotion of electronic machines. Still, the respect for reason remains strong enough to enable most readers to voice the old objections against a claim like that of Walter Van Tilburg Clark: you write of sprites and mountain hikes and mystic black painters, suggesting a reality beyond reason; but what objective check is there on your knowledge beyond reason? Granted you may feel such things as substantive, by what standard do you say this supposed reality is a part of *my* life too?

The Watchful Gods is an appropriate test case. It received mixed reviews, but was generally conceded to have been written with skill and sensitivity. The major objections that were made by reviewers consisted almost entirely of doubts about the objective validity of Clark's story of a twelve-year-old boy and a rabbit hunt.[2] The subsequent critical neglect of the novelette is the typical fate of works thought to have been well written but lacking the universal quality we associate with enduring literature. *The Watchful Gods*, I hope to demonstrate, does contain permanent meaning; and it does dramatize, in the form of an internal debate, the objectivity of a knowledge which is outside the domain of reason, a knowledge which is at least as honorable as the more prestigious workings of conscious reason.

I   *An American Schoolboy and the Eternal Return*

The most obvious thing about *The Watchful Gods* is that it is a fictive study of sacred unity. Buck, the boy-hero of the story, is very much filled with a sense of the sacrality of life. His ritual swims, naked in the sea; his sense of a secret and holy place; and his vivid images of the unity and multiplicity of life represent the characteristics of a sacred imagination. Buck is, nonetheless, very much a part of his contemporary and American world. He is a tennis fan, he hero-worships the cool prizefighter, he reads romantic books typical of young readers of his time; if "compelled to discuss God," he "would have spoken in . . . standard Protestant-go-to-Sunday-school terms"; [3] and he wants more than anything to receive for his twelfth birthday the .22-caliber rifle which hangs on pegs in his father's study. When the important day arrives, Buck strides forth, alone, on his first real hunt—only to find the two worlds crashing in on him. His prey, as it turns out, is not a ferocious beast, but a rabbit, a baby rabbit at that. And the unbearable irony is that he shoots badly, chopping away at a small animal too shocked to run. Overcome with grief and shame, Buck conducts a funeral for his victim.

Less obvious than the fact that both sacred and profane realities exist in Buck's world are the conditions under which unity is possible. These conditions are not easy to see, I think, because they run counter to our culturally imbued expectations. In a profane world view, in that generally individualistic and activist value system which characterizes modern life, one is required to adhere to reason or to reject reason. If reason is admitted as a valid standard, it is admitted as the supreme standard; and thus putting reason aside, on occasions of faith, is considered arbitrary. An exception is permitted only when the primacy of reason is granted a proper deference, and thus is no exception after all. The typical Protestant, for example, may reject reason and believe on the basis of faith, but the rationale offered in justification of the rejection is itself an effort in reason. In a sacred world view, however, it is possible to admit the legitimacy of reason without holding it supreme. Reason, it is felt, should be used when it applies; but to make it the supreme standard of knowing is to

deny the world by trying to reduce the infinite to a tiny intellectual knot small enough to fit into man's brain.[4]

Buck's problem, since he is living an American life, is a very
common one: how do you relate sense experience to principles;
how do you get content into the forms of knowledge and thus
discover a unity within multiplicity? As an initiate into sacrality,
however, Buck sees the problem in atypical language. In his
terms, the variety of life is signaled by realities: a "fog god,"
which he associates vaguely with the Old Testament God; and
"sprites," which he feels are more compatible with Jesus Christ.
The fog god is force, duty, iron justice, as well as the indifferent
energies of nature and death. The sprites are the joy of being
alive, the moment of ecstasy. Between the two, and in fact within
either one, there is no discoverable rational unity. The Old Testament God is to Buck an inconsistent deity who is "dangerously
and incalculably whimsical." The God who selected the "ribald,
drunken, fleshly" (201) Noah to save the world, Buck thinks,
cannot be the same God who "quietly and gently walked with
the good Ruth at sunset" (201–2). Nor can either of these Old
Testament Gods be called, on rational grounds, the same God
who "amused himself by giving Adam his beloved companion
Eve, and then, just when everything should have been happiest,
doomed them with the smiling little apple trick, as if their tran-
quil drama bored Him" (202).

Buck's reasoning about God has its comic element, but his
thoughts are neither juvenile nor aberrant. It would be easy to
compile a long list of substantial thinkers who, like Buck, have
been deeply disturbed by the inability of the rational mind to
account for God's actions. This disturbingly irrational God, is,
in Clark's view, an ironic concoction of man's rational affinity
for absolutes and consistency: two plus two will *always* equal
four, and it is good that this is so. God, it is felt, should enjoy
similar virtues of consistency and perfection. Since goodness is
desirable, God should be all good and only good. Proceeding in
this fashion, man's reason concocted a God felt to be omnipotent,
omniscient, and benevolent, and deemed Him the sole ruler of
a world in which babies could be born deformed and innocents
could be murdered and mutilated by plagues and earthquakes,
a world in which unequal opportunity to be saved was a historical fact. The Protestant-go-to-Sunday-school God, then, is

made out of modern man's ideas about rational consistency rather than the felt-thought of actual experience. Reason is simply unable to accommodate the love, indifference, and hate which come into life with cosmic authority. The result of confining God's possibilities to human reason is a Protestant-go-to-Sunday-school God who does not represent what we see in the universe or feel within ourselves. He can be felt only on Sunday, only in the special circumstances of a church walled off from the eminent irrationalities of daily life.

Buck, with the integrity of innocence, cannot be content with a God (or a unity) that is fit only for perfunctory worship on hollow Sundays. The very essence of sacrality is the felt-presence of God in the workaday world. Thus unity, in order to be realistic rather than abstracted, must include the inconsistent energies of God and the disparate voices of one's inner self. This is why the sacred man reasons when he can, yet bases his hopes for unity on the image-thinking capacities of the unconscious. Buck has a proper respect for this hope, but he is a sacred child, not a sacred man; and he has much to learn. Primarily, he has not yet gone beyond the vague suspicion that his sprites and his moments of ecstasy are just as isolated from total life as the intellectualized God of his Sunday school.

II   *The Great Tennis Match: Dream and Promise*

In part, Buck is groping for a language. He uses the terms that are available to him, and neither "God" nor "Jesus" is an accurate term. "Old Testament God," for example, represents his readings in the Old Testament and his experiences at church, and yet somehow includes parental authority and the .22-caliber rifle. Still, his respect for an indifferent universal force is a hopeful sign. He is right in seeing that the Old Testament God, however "dark and uncertain," is real, even "more convincing" (202) than the God of the New Testament; and Buck will not deny the Old God for the convenience of his rational expectations. He is right, also, to see that the gods of joy are suspiciously pure, insubstantial, and too arbitrarily invoked. That which is "real only in the moments of ecstasy" (203) cannot be remembered accurately by the conscious mind, can only be felt by celebrations of the body in dance. Buck is evasive about this limitation, for it is only after shooting the rabbit that he begins to learn the role of conscious reason in sacred experience.

The limitation would be no problem at all for one whose sacred quest was nostalgic, hinged to romantic dreams of the Orient; but Clark's young hero, as I have suggested above, is not seeking an escapist sacrality. Like Hal Bridges, he is in and of his time and place. Sacred unity will have to include the fog god and the sprites; and it will have to include an academic but much-loved father, an affectionate but somewhat cloying mother, and a sister who condescends with infuriating skill; and it cannot ignore the barrenness of a modernity which is nonetheless his own, the necessity and the terror of growing from boyhood into manhood without the counsel of cultural ceremony. Buck knows there is something sacred about the changes he is undergoing in this his twelfth year, but there are no modern rites of passage. He will have to journey alone.

This is the reason that Buck's adolescent worship of the primordial has to make do with insubstantial stuff. When the story opens, Buck has just awakened from a dream. His mind grabs back "like a hand" (191), like one trying to remember with the felt-thoughts of the unconscious mind. But a felt-thought has a vitality of its own, an autonomy not within the compass of the reason; and Buck is not yet mature about the internal debate he is soon to face: the dream "skittered out from under his memory" (191), that is, moved with its own animal volition away from the empirical domain of his now-awakened conscious mind.

This seemingly innocent beginning foreshadows the central meaning of the story. Buck's initiation is an early lesson in learning to think with the unconscious, as with a hand, and in doing so with a realistic awareness of the legitimate voice of the conscious mind. His aptness as a pupil is shown by the way his mind works. He thinks in terms of place, shapes, things, movement; and he tries to mold it all into a unified picture. As he begins to dream—in his conscious mind now—he falls into Walter Mitty heroics; but the strategies of his dreams are favorable promises for his future: he assigns himself a role selected because it "fitted in so much better" (192) with thoughts gathered by his imagination. The particulars of this imagination are "a thousand glittering fragments," "tiny, multiple flashings of minnows," "the grains of beach sand," "drops of . . . radiant mist" (194). Such terms, for one who believes in the primacy of the rational mind, would be the language of an escapist romanticism. For Buck, who is learning the primacy of the unconscious mind, this is a language far more realistic than the abstractions of man's delimiting intellect.

That childish type of romanticism which is a part of Buck is not shown by his finding that the multiple flashings of the sprites are "all allied . . . in the glad meaning of life" (194), for that discovery is a sign of his proper apprenticeship to sacrality. His youthful romanticism *is* shown by comic efforts to control his inner self in the world of the fog god and in the workaday world of actuality. The entire story, in fact, is an account of the various ways in which Buck tries to see that things are "fitted in" as they ought to be. This is the chief characteristic of the account of his daydreams, his desire for the rifle, his relations with his father, his efforts to move or speak in a certain way, the hopes that his sister Evelyn will not spoil things with her teasing and condescension, his determination not to let his mother's good intentions goad him into unmanly displays of childish or imbalanced emotions, his plan to give the wooden gun to his little brother Arthur in the right way, his ritualistic standards for killing properly, and—finally—his ceremonial and psychological efforts to discover whatever balance may be possible for a sacred boy who has felt the shocking burden of sacred manhood. The entire story, in short, is a study of inner balance held precariously and in romanticized forms, then lost, and finally regained through the realization that the old ways will never work again, that joy from now on will be harder come by.

Buck's initiation, which follows very closely the steps analyzed by Arnold Van Gennep in *Rites of Passage,* is described at first in a style marked by affection and irony. In one daydream, Buck seeks "to escape from the dangerous toils of an Isolt of Ireland who was a good deal like Alice Gladding, who had sat in the row beside him, but two seats ahead, during the last school year" (198). Buck does not "use the saints very often" in his daydreams "because it was almost impossible to work a heroine in with a saint in a manner that was at all satisfying and still keep the saint much of a saint" (205). For weeks Buck has moved about in the "nonchalant but guarded manner, which approximated, he believed, the relaxed and confident advance of a skilled boxer from his corner" (209). At times, Buck comes upon "one of those rare, realistic moments in which he was forced to admit that he had never spoken one word to the real Janet Haley, and probably never would" (223).

Nevertheless, Buck pushes aside this annoying intrusion of realism and constructs in his mind a tale of heroism which has all the characteristics of a melodrama. He is vague about details, especially when some mere fact gets in the way of imaginative heroics; and he shifts his and Janet's ages about for his own convenience. The dream centers around a monumental tennis match in which he defeats a "licentious old expert in an exhausting, five-set final before such a multitude as probably only the Rose Bowl could have seated, with Janet, by an evil, pre-match agreement into which Buck had somehow been trapped, as the real trophy" (223). All of the details are melodramatic and exaggerated; and they are just as characteristic of the youthful Buck as are his imaginative responses to the sacrality of his secret place on the beach. Not yet able to attain a realistically sacred balance, Buck has channeled primordial energies into the melodrama of a modish value system, and he is due for a shock. When the test comes—and it inevitably will come—he will find that his understanding of unity is tenuous, not yet tough enough to deal with a reality which includes both the sacred and the profane.

III   *The Methodology of Watching Gods*

Buck has not yet learned the meaning Clark points to with his title: the gods are watchful. In earlier and more purely primitive forms of sacrality, it is permissible to fool the gods; but Clark has accepted the emphasis on will forced upon him by American history. To trick the gods, therefore, is to trick one's self. Buck, whose youth puts him closer to primitive sacrality, thinks it is permissible to fool the fog god. That he is mistaken is shown by the tricks and moral evasions he tries to work on his parents. As he tries to fool the fog god, so does he try to fool his father. As he tells a half-lie to his mother about a forbidden swim, so does he tell a half-lie to himself. The parents, obviously, are not fooled; and neither is the fog god.

The gods are watchful because modern man has developed

both his consciousness and his conscience; and, in so doing, has internalized the gods. They see that Buck's dreams are not built with care when a detail proves troublesome—such as how Buck as the perfect dream-hero could have been fooled into gambling at tennis for Janet Haley—and they see the absurdity of Buck's hints, swaggers, poses. The guilt, of course, is venial; for Buck is but a boy. His Kit Carson manner is comic. It is his Kit Carson manner, however, which he takes with him, and which deserts him, when he moves into the actual killing of game. The only one who is fooled is Buck himself.

When Buck shoots the rabbit, he experiences the disorientation which marks the hunter who has despoiled the ritual of the hunt. Sensations of the globe, of space unhinged, swing into his consciousness. Distances are deceptive. He sees and feels distortions. His child's vision of unity has cracked under the first pressure. Desperately wanting to recover some sense of place and being, he experiences an eagerness to "lay hands upon his first kill" (260). Encouraged, he feeds his eagerness "with fragments of worldly maxim and bits of thick-skinned, male, public attitude," a mistake that is basic to his disorientation. The eagerness to touch his first kill blends in with its source, the illusions of his dreams and poses, and cannot be brought to bear upon the primordial reality (which is at once sacred and brutish) that he has just confronted. When he comes to the rabbit, his "too-widespread defiance [is] no longer able to sustain him at all" (260–261). As the shock comes full upon him, his initiation into primordial reality has begun: "all unknown to him, the enormous, primal chaos engendered by his act slowly shrank and was reshaped toward reality" (261).

The internal debate, heard first when Buck aims at the rabbit, now begins in earnest. There is a "rebellion within the congress of his insides" (263). But confrontation with the primordial is painful, and Buck's consciousness bumbles before the enormity of his feelings. He wants to make himself "attentive to nothing going on inside himself, but only to the safe, fixed things about him" (264). But the gods, at least for an initiate into sacrality, are watchful. The description of the way in which they watch is basic to the story's central meaning: "He looked around quickly, feeling that he wasn't alone in the ravine or on the bench-land, that somewhere, not very near, but near enough, certainly, to see him and be curious and perhaps even to guess, there was a man standing, a quiet, watchful, judging man, almost, but not quite, a stranger. There was no man, though. The watching was there, but not the man to do it" (264).

In part, no man is there to do the watching because primordial meaning exists whether or not we know it, exists regardless of the mutilations of modern abstractions about religion. In part, no man is there because the stranger who is not quite a stranger is Buck himself. But the watching goes on, most fundamentally, because sacred man in modern times—with his non-mystical emphasis on individual ego, free will, and responsibility—has assigned himself the nervous duty of establishing a personal relation with impersonal gods. And thus occur the voices of the inner debate, the "rebellion within the congress of his insides," for the various counselors of this congress must be represented; a balance in tension must be sought. No longer can Buck enjoy a playlike sense of unity. The act of killing has opened his eyes to the primal chaos, to the fog god in a primordial rather than in a merely Biblical form. As Buck begins to sense the awesome difference between the original God and the story-book God, he begins to learn the discipline that is far more realistic and profound than all the rules of reason.

Buck, to put it bluntly, is learning that the voices of his own inner debate will discipline one another: sacred feelings allowed to become unrealistic fall thereby within the realm of reason and are subject to its admonitions; reason that becomes arrogant or too abstract or too much a matter of cheap male ego can in turn be admonished by the welling up from within, perhaps in violent shapes, of man's inner sense of the primordial. On the story level, this elementary principle of the discipline is shown in Buck's desire to flee from the terror of reality and return to the innocence of his secret beach. He has "lost the bright gods" (268) of innocence, has "not been accepted by the dark," feels himself in "no soul's land" (268), and wants his innocence back again—just as he wants the rabbit to come alive again.

The narrative sequence of life, however, unlike the sequence of events in a daydream, will not revoke itself for the convenience of a troubled conscience. The "unquestionable death" of the rabbit is for Buck a harsh lesson in elementary realism. More important is his feeling of being watched on the secret beach.

The watcher, he discovers, is "inescapable" though impossible to discover. Like Curt and the black painter in *The Track of the Cat*, Buck and his watcher represent an epiphany. Both Curt and Buck feel pursued; both feel the watcher is first on this side, then on the other. Neither the cat nor the watcher is to be taken in Freudian terms, that is, as illusions created out of repressions. Both are to be taken, rather, in Jungian terms, as projections of archetypal realities through the image-thinking capacities of the unconscious; distorted, it is true, but distorted into truth. Buck, a better student than Curt, is learning that he cannot flee the primordial, not by running to his secret beach or to any other special place. One of the voices he carries with him, wherever he goes, is the silent voice of primordial reality, the presence more powerful than words. For those who play with wooden guns, made-up images are an adequate rationale, just as half-lies are close enough to the truth; those who kill with real guns will find themselves in desperate need of a sterner discipline.

Unable to flee, Buck begins his apprenticeship in ceremony, in ritual. It is an awkward process, for "he-man" hunters do not bury rabbits. That, to a reasoning society, would be silly. Yet when Buck works toward a proper respect for killing, toward some sympathy with the sacrality of blood as real and irrevocable blood, and begins to feel the rabbit in himself and himself in the rabbit, then he is learning a realistic unity. Even the simple act of shifting the rabbit to a more comfortable position gives him a knowledge beyond the capacities of the intellect. The burial, however, though a favorable sign for Buck's sacred character, is not the resolution of the story. Having completed the ceremony, Buck comes to feel that the funeral is "a grim, necessary and inadequate penance" (285). The reason for the inadequacy, I think, underscores the most essential principle of inner discipline.

IV   *The Role of the Rational Mind in a Sacred Vision*

The inner debate about the burial is characterized by intellectual distinctions that are careful enough to interest a philosopher. One discrimination follows another until Buck's innermost will is thoroughly parted, layer from layer, and exposed. The academic and stilted language of the debaters is directly comparable to that used later in the essay-story "The Writer and the

Professor," a piece supposedly written long after Clark's peda-
gogical commitments had "first" introduced him to a concern
with the critical intellect. It would be more accurate, I think,
to say that Clark, as an honest student of the American experience, was deeply interested in modern man's tormenting intellect
before he began to publish. Certainly, the point made by the
debate is an incisive probing of the will behind the burial: is
Buck planning to bury the rabbit for the sake of the rabbit, as a
religious act of contrition; or is he planning to hide his own
shame?

The agreement reached between "counsel for the world" and
"counsel for burial," to Buck's embarrassment, is founded on two
non-sacred lines of argument. First, the "defendant's manliness"
cannot "be demonstrated to women in the eyeless corpse of a
rabbit no bigger than his two hands"; second, the defendant
cannot demonstrate his skill to his father, "unquestionably an
excellent marksman, by exhibiting in the ears of that tiny rabbit,
the holes made by two cruel and clumsy shots which failed to
kill" (292). Motives based on fear of the standards of male ego,
of course, taint an act of sacrality; and Buck knows it. He is
"unable to deny, under the burden of his [the primordial judge's]
eyes, that the agreement, though it permitted the better action,
had been arrived at by the most despicable means" (292–93). The
words "unable to deny" suggest, furthermore, that both author
and hero are aware of this judgment and that it is a valid judgment.

The burial, then, is not at bottom a sacred act. It has value
because Buck realizes it is the "better action" and because he
tries to make it come off; but he buries the rabbit out of shame
for having killed a baby instead of a full-grown rabbit, out of
shame for having butchered the rabbit instead of killing it
cleanly, and in fear of the taunts of male-ego values as represented by the eyes of his family.

Buck has a clear understanding of his weak and tainted will,
and the voices of academic reasoning in his consciousness are
cool and analytical. Clearly, Clark's boy-hero is not simply an
innocent primitive. As his promise of development is shown by
the sacred characteristics of his imagination—his use of place,
shape, and balance—so is his doom shown by the analytical habits
and by the rightness of his conscious intellect. The subject of the

story, therefore, is not exotic. Buck's complex imagination, though different, is comparable to that of Hawthorne's Hester and Dimmesdale, Melville's Ishmael and Captain Vere, Hemingway's Jake Barnes and Frederic Henry, Faulkner's Quentin Compson and Ike McCaslin. Clark's study of a driven and painfully analytical consciousness finds its rationale in a world view more primordial than that of mainline American novelists, but his concern with the rational will and the moral responsibilities of the individual and his concern with the dark realities of nonrational meaning are germane to the history of American letters. Central to his contribution to that general concern with the rational and the mysterious is his work toward a disciplined relation between the two.

Our understanding of Clark needs a fuller recognition of the importance of the rational in his vision of man. It is, I want to emphasize, the disturbingly academic voices of Buck's conscious intellect which expose the flaw in his religious ceremony. These pedantic voices can speak with historical and psychological authority if not with ontological authority. They cannot deal generatively with the archetypal material of the unconscious, with meanings that come from the primordial, or expect the primordial to constrict itself to man's understanding; but they can deal with the ethical materials of man's conscious mind and with voices from the primordial as they speak to the conscious mind; and they can do so with a capability far beyond the passive role Jung assigned to reason.

Buck is not wrong to let the voices of reason speak; his need for further growth *is* suggested by the fact that they speak without paying attention to him. There is mockery in the way they refer to Buck as the defendant, as if he had nothing to say about the arguments of his own consciousness; and the tone is appropriate. Buck has allowed himself to be guided too much by the values of male ego, the values of the world mockingly represented by the intellectual voices of his counselors; and the result is that he has spoiled the hunt and the effort in atonement represented by the burial.

Buck has not achieved a mature and realistic version of sacred unity. He can still hide behind the childish images of the cool prizefighter. He has evaded his real decision about manhood, about the place of the fog god and the sprites in his future life;

and he falls again into the guilt of the partly hypocritical and partly holy burial of the rabbit (see the paragraph at the bottom of 298). Still, he is not yet far into the first day of his twelfth year; he does realize that he is not "going home," back to Kit Carson innocence; he has admitted to himself the legitimate role of the rational mind in its comments on the conscious will behind his efforts in sacrality; and he does go on with the burial despite all his counselors, fear, guilt—and this is genuine testimony to his recognition of the primary authority of the dictates of the unconscious. He is beginning to learn the discipline of the inner debate.

CHAPTER 7

Homunculus in the Twentieth Century: Poems, Stories, and a Brief Assessment

WHATEVER Clark may write in the future, he has come to the end of a period in his career. He is too honest a craftsman to repeat what he has already done, and further accomplishments will have to come from fresh sources. It is appropriate, then, to assess the relevance of what he has accomplished. His productive period divides into two distinct parts, the poetry of the 1930's and the fiction of the 1940's. A comparison of the poetry and the short stories, in the light of the 1962 essay-story entitled "The Writer and the Professor," provides a convenient means of suggesting the place of Clark in literary history and of evaluating his relevance to the lives of contemporary readers.

I *Apprenticeship in Poetry*

For Clark, as for Hemingway and Faulkner and many other novelists, the writing of poems was an apprenticeship for the writing of fiction. His poems, I think, are minor; but writing them was preparation for more mature work, and reading them enables us to study Clark's development as an artist. *Ten Women in Gale's House and Shorter Poems*, Clark's 1932 volume of poems, is a noteworthy example of "primary realism," the attempt to discover an esthetic shape for the belief that thought and things are one.

The first poem in the volume reveals an interest in the abstract and thus contrasts with the concretions of the fiction. "The Death of Chuang Tsu, The Wise One," falls into poetry of statement; but those statements depict with overt clarity Clark's abiding interest in Eastern thinking. Confucius comes to Chuang Tsu,

who is dying, to hear his last words of wisdom; but Chuang Tsu
does not believe knowledge can be taught:

> "I have nothing I can teach you.
> Man must learn of his own life.
> If I might I would not teach you.
> You have not been true to wisdom
> Confucius.
> You have given laws to men
> Whereupon to order life.
> Know you not the laws are given?
> Knowledge of them comes from within." [1]

The idea is repeated throughout the poem:

> "You cannot give them, else
> They should not be The Laws." (10)
>
> . . . .
> "The Laws are, and are found
> Within." (11)
>
> . . . .
> "You cannot teach men wisdom
> Confucius." (11)

Since the laws cannot be taught, reason is ruled out as a means
to ultimate knowing. The laws are internal, within each person;
and they cannot be codified or formulated. Knowledge, nonetheless, is objective in the sense that it is not man's arbitrary or personal creation. What man must do, Chuang Tsu suggests, is to
awaken within himself an awareness of the larger reality of
which he is a part. He must observe:

> "If one would watch
> The flight of the wild duck and
> The rippling of water about
> The reed stems
> He would know more
> Than rules can teach him." (11)

This same thought appears in the short story called "Chuangtse
and the Prince of the Golden Age" and in more typical stories

of the sensitive young hunter who locks eyeballs with his quarry and freezes, shocked by the recognition of a kinship which is beyond rational analysis.[2] The cool accomplishment of a Chuang Tsu, however, is denied the American. In "Youth Seeks for Truth," the values are those of Chuang Tsu, but the torment is that of the American who is wracked by worldly "desire," a word which occurs six times in the poem.

Clark's concern with Eastern values is in an American grain, and one thinks of comparisons. Emerson's most famous essays call for a welding of universal values and the individual experiences of the individual American—but his plea was for a unity we did not have. Whitman wrote *Leaves of Grass*, a paean to mystical unity; but he also wrote *Democratic Vistas*, decrying our lack of unity. Typical, also, is literature in which a non-American or a non-white American achieves a unity denied those who belong to the main stream of the American experience (Steinbeck's peasants are good examples). When an American comes close to the achievement of unity, he is an outcast, a misfit, or he is a cultural adjunct who observes but seldom participates. Steinbeck, in his portrait of John Wayne in *To a God Unknown*, again provides a good example; and in Clark's *The Track of the Cat* it is Hal who must save the ranch, not Arthur, whose chief role is that of nay-sayer or priest. Eastern unity, then, functions in Clark's poetry and to some extent in his fiction as a peace denied those who sold the promise of America and reduced the land to commercial realities merely. In the poetry, however, the emphasis is on Oriental rather than Jungian parallels, and this changing emphasis is basic to Clark's development.

Perhaps the most recurrent image in Clark's short poems, for example, is that of the soul as a prisoner in the body. For the strict Eastern mystic, the desired solution is unmistakable. The body is a puny container, temporary and unimportant, useful only as a tool to serve the soul's dedication to unity with the ultimate. For the mystic damaged by the American experience, however, to deny the integrity of the physical as an end in itself is to deny one's own history, is to betray the burden of America's democratic dedication to the practical.

Later, in the fiction, Clark shifted from his American version of mysticism to his American version of sacrality; but his long poem, "Ten Women in Gale's House," is an early study of a cultural burden which—from one viewpoint or another—has concerned him throughout his career. Gale, a painter whose house suggests Robinson Jeffers' Thor House, invites the speaker to view his ten women, his ten great paintings. Each portrait represents a different type of woman, a different set of values. Elizabeth represents propriety, modernity, materialism. Helen represents a cool wisdom, Jacqueline is passion, and Aunt Ellen personifies domestic warmth, the simple and trusting love of family. These and others are meant to be symbolic, so alive and concrete that Gale and his guest must often escape to the next painting or else be overwhelmed and lost. For the reader of the poem, however, they remain allegorical. The poem, in short, is not well conceived; the strategy forces it toward preachment. Instead of talking about truth in the abstract, Gale and his visitor discuss truth as represented by the portraits; but the portraits are a thin veil over a philosophical motive. They are not an adequate objective correlative. The attitudes expressed, however, are significant as instances of what Clark had to work through in order to get to *The Ox-Bow Incident.*

The cool wisdom of Elizabeth is much admired by Gale and the speaker, but it is a wisdom lacking in practicality. Gale lives in the world, and—however much the world outside his studio may consist of a horn-honking, money-grabbing reality—it is nonetheless out there; and it is the place in which people live their lives. The passionate Jacqueline, by contrast, is too much of vitality. If one stays too long in her presence, he "might forget the sea" (45) and the infinity it represents. Aunt Ellen, whose love is instant and genuine, provides relief for the artist who is caught between the wisdom of Elizabeth and the passion of Jacqueline; but Aunt Ellen reminds Gale of the times when he was a small boy in trouble and there was an Aunt Ellen to treat a scratched knee or feed a hungry tummy or soothe hurt feelings. She is very real and very warm, but she is a comfort, not a resolution. Aunt Ellen ministers to boys, not to men.

The rest of the poem develops this theme. Different types of beauty appear, different approaches to truth; but each one is somehow flawed, in some way limited. The portraits can teach, but they cannot answer the questions of the man who is caught in a prison of flesh and yet hears the infinity of the sea; nor can they resolve his torment. The final portrait, death, suggests that life is a small and temporal offshoot of a transcendental reality. Then the image of the child returns, with the relation of this world to the ultimate being compared to the relation of a baby to a wise father. Gale and the speaker in the poem reach a sardonic conclusion: they doubt that the world outside the studio is real, but they "must try."

Dedicated to the most concrete and to the most abstract, Walter Clark was groping for an objective correlative to shape the horror and the beauty of the land that lay between, the land that was both actual and real and yet neither, the land of paradox in which man must live. In *The Ox-Bow Incident* he was to find his way, but in the early poetry of the 1930's he was too concerned with abstractions and with the theme of lost or endangered purity, themes that have tempted and tormented—and usually misled—many writers associated with the American West.

II   *The Relevance of the Authentic Western*

Clark's development toward objectivity and sacrality is suggested by poems like "Strength of Autumn End" and "Of the Broken Brotherhood" and by short stories like "Hook" and "The Rise and the Passing of Bar." [3] In part, the change is a shift from overtly Oriental themes to disciplined studies of the land itself. In part, the change represents Clark's discovery of his own place in the Western experience. Voices representing the West, of course, are so bewildering in their variety that conjectures about influence are exceedingly dangerous. Anything close to a full bibliography of the West would have to include such diverse figures as Roy Rogers, Laotse, John Steinbeck, Robert Bly, Frederick Jackson Turner, Andy Adams, James Fenimore Cooper, Big Foot Wallace, Vardis Fisher, Theodore Roosevelt, Frederick Manfred, J. Frank Dobie, Wallace Stevens, Walt Whitman, and Billy the Kid. Questions of influence aside, however, there is a helpful comparison to be made between Clark's development as an artist and the characteristic themes of Western writing generally.

Fundamental among studies of Western writing is Mody C. Boatright's analysis of the literature of the cattle complex: writing which is devoted to experiences and values directly related to the cattle industry.[4] The identifying characteristic of such writing is a devotion to historical validity while maintaining a deep interest in the meaning (often the mythic meaning) of a very personal human experience. The preeminent spokesman of this segment of Western literature is J. Frank Dobie, Texas historian and folklorist. In scores of books, like *The Mustangs* and *A Vaquero of the Brush Country*, he has given shape to the facts as well as to the meanings of life in the cow country. His works, founded in personal experience as a cowhand and rancher, are disciplined by extensive studies of folklore, by careful research, and by an integrity of character which was remarkably unswerving. Dobie's wide experience and learning, it must be emphasized, are not devoted to a mere recording. He was always at work to discover an idea, to unfold the meaning of a vast experience. "If I have idealized the horse," he writes, "I have not overestimated his importance in social history: the climax of horse riding in America was the climax of free enterprise of the frontier kind." The possibility of becoming a cowboy, for many, was the possibility of becoming a free man. "The rule," Dobie continues, "is simple: the more machinery man gets, the more machined he is. When the traveler got off a horse and into a machine, the tempo of his mind as well as of his locomotion was changed." [5]

A similar concern is evident in the two bibles of cowboy literature, Andy Adams' *The Log of a Cowboy* and Charles Siringo's *A Texas Cowboy*, both works of documentary fiction written out of the actual experiences of early cowhands. The blunt power of these two books has seldom been approached by their successors. Owen Wister and Eugene Manlove Rhodes are good, but they are steps toward Jack Schaefer and scores of lesser authors who write not of the historical West but of the Hollywood prefabrication. The literature of the cattle complex, beginning as does all good regional literature with an attempt to give universal shape to local experience, has been hurt—in reputation—by those who fail to distinguish the genuine article from the Hollywood imitation. The genuine tradition has nonetheless been available for those with the proper affinity.

Clark, as we can see by comparing the early poetry to the later short stories, has that affinity. His writing is *not* literature of the cattle complex certainly, but his early poetic explorations of perfection were changed by experiences (if not by readings) related to that tradition; and the result was his American version of sacrality. With this development—most clearly seen in *The Ox-Bow Incident*—Clark forged his own place in literary history.[6]

III *Nostalgia and Tension*

The frontier, though not Clark's overt subject, is germane to an understanding of what he has accomplished. The frontier in American literary history has long been associated with the American dream, the promised land, the garden of America, and with a variety of ideas about the loss of the dream, the betrayal of innocence, the despoiling and commercialization of the last Eden. Perhaps the most recurrent idea is that frontier experience is representative of the conflict between nature and civilization, between an idealized or at least idyllic innocence and the realistic necessities of progress. James Fenimore Cooper is a typical reference point, and Clark is supposed to owe a great deal to Cooper and to others who have dramatized the corruption of the natural life of the frontier by the encroachments of an inexorable civilization. I hope it does not sound cantankerous, therefore, when I say I cannot believe there is any significant relation between such themes and the fiction of Walter Clark. If Clark had continued in the vein suggested by his poetry, the comparison would have been apt; but because of Clark's dedication to the land— in a way that is comparable to the genuine cowboy tradition —he became less concerned with the pure and the abstract, less concerned with the natural innocence which fascinated Cooper, Rousseau, Whitman, and others. Henry James and Henry Adams, I believe it can be shown, are more relevant to Clark's fiction than James Fenimore Cooper.

Post-Eisenhower leaders in Washington have impressed television and newspaper correspondents as the new breed, as men born in the twentieth century and thus born to pressure. Leaders like President John Kennedy and President Lyndon Johnson are said never to have known the peace of the pre-World War I period or to have dreamed of a return to such days. Tension is thought to be the chief condition of existence, and the primary question is what can be accomplished within tension. Something like this, in a curious way, is basic to the sensibilities of Walter Clark and of several other Western novelists of his own generation. Clark was not around when the frontier was innocent, un-

despoiled. Civilization had moved in, and hopes of an American
Eden had been crushed long before Walter Clark reached the age
of apprehension. Appropriately, none of his stories, as I read
them, deals with Cooper's frontier.[7] Clark's most representative
story, certainly, is of a modern man who discovers—often in
shocking ways—the frontier within himself, the homunculus that
civilization has not yet obliterated in any man. Clark does write
of the innocence of youth, but he makes no association between
the purity of the young and the purity of nature before civilization. He writes of a youthful innocence which might be found in
almost any time or place.

It follows that Clark's fictive heroes do not try to rediscover or
to return to a historical state they have never known. That which
is lost was lost centuries ago, and the victims are frontiersmen
as well as sophisticated residents of the "moribund city." Note
that it is Gerald Tetley (the rich town boy) and not Art Croft
(the cowboy writer) who is most aware of the primordial, and
that Art Bridges' sacrality is associated with reading as well as
with nature. Two of Clark's most sacred heroes are Tim Hazard
and Buck, and both are modern, both of the city, both readers
of medieval romance, and both have to learn that the nature of
Cooper and the innocence of Rousseau are not just violations of
practicality but, rather, violations of sacred reality.

The challenge, then, is not to return to an earlier point in linear
time. The challenge is to feel in the ancient memories of cyclical
time the present throb of primordial meaning. There is, consequently, a skip between religious act and felt result, a skip which
seems evasive and equivocal to readers who have been taught
that communication is a panacea (American students believe that
a professor who will have a beer with you, in his own kitchen,
is a professor who will give you an "A"; Americans generally
believe that all arguments are word arguments). But for Clark
the religious act of living this life is primitive in the sense that
one should feel archetypal powers, shape the resultant energies
within himself, try to behave with respect, and then wait. Later,
you will find out how well you have done. A profane man expects
his God to behave according to man's reasoned notion of communication: if he worships sincerely, he has done his part; and
God ought then to do His, ought in some way to respond. Sacred
man, however, does not worship in this sense. He tries to propi-

tiate the gods, but not to presume an answer; for the primordial gods are malevolent and indifferent, as well as benevolent.

IV *Inviolate Archetypes: The Short Stories*

Within this context we can understand "Hook," one of Clark's best-known short stories. "Hook" is an unusual story in that its power is undeniable; and yet the main character, almost the only character, is a hawk. The reader feels himself deeply moved, but is hard put to say why he is. The power of the story, I think, lies in its dramatic presentation of archetypal energies. Hook feels three profound sensations: the "joy of space," the "joy of battle," and, because circumstances frustrate him, the hunger rather than the joy of love.[8] In a world in which God must be understood, the story of Hook is too abstract, seems to have no relevance to the lives of actual men; but in a world in which the gods must be propitiated, the mere touch of archetypal energies is an eminently practical matter; and this—Clark would feel—is why the hawk's story can stir ancient memories even in a sophisticated reader. "The Wind and the Snow of Winter," by contrast, is much closer to the nostalgia often associated with stories of the West and, indeed, is saved from sentimentality only by a most diligent restraint.

"The Rapids" and "Why Don't You Look Where You're Going?" are not intended to be major stories—both are a kind of fictive joke—but Clark's characteristic values are clearly revealed. In "The Rapids," a businessman from the world of Babbitt (his boss is called D.L.) is on a brief vacation in the woods. Strolling off by himself, he spots a waterlogged old boat overturned in the water. Suddenly he is seized with a sense of adventure. Energies which have long been dormant are awakened (Sherwood Anderson is a relevant comparison). Pride, courage, and determination spring to life in his comic efforts to recover and navigate the boat. He is obviously willing to risk life and limb in the project, until suddenly his wife, the voice of civilization, intrudes with annoyed incomprehension: the boss wants him back in town at once. His wife wonders what possessed him to behave so oddly, and he of course is petulantly unable and unwilling to explain. Heading back to the moribund trap, he has "to clutch at his dressing gown tightly, to keep it from streaming out and leaving him uncovered" (64). The man, of course, has been uncovered; and what he seeks to hide is more than physical nakedness. Beneath the thin veneer of city life lies the homunculus that is in us all, even if he does emerge only at rare times, only in pathetic and foolish ways.

In "Why Don't You Look Where You're Going?" the dormant power of homunculus also emerges to surprise the world of civilization. "White as a sainted leviathan, but too huge for even God to have imagined it" (113), an ocean liner moves eastward, with everyone on board "comfortable, even satisfied" (113). The tongue-in-cheek tone of the story warns against an elaborate interpretation, but the ocean liner is nonetheless an allegorical representation of modern civilization. An "ordinary mortal" feels no responsibility for himself when riding such an overwhelming structure, certainly "he could not do anything about it"; but what is most comforting is that "he could not be expected to do anything about it" (113). Complacency and comfort in the mass and machinery of modern structures produces the contentment of a dull child.

The characters—who are referred to anonymously, Stephen Crane fashion, as the "moustached man," "the young man"—play a petty game of one-upsmanship when a tiny object is spotted in the distance. Each one strives in casual pomposity to be the hero in the game of identification. The object turns out to be a small boat, absurdly in the middle of the ocean, with a single occupant. The liner nearly runs him down, but the boatman swerves just in time, then shakes both fists at the enormous liner and screams: "Why don't you look where you're going?" The passengers find that their skin-deep world has been penetrated: they chortle in delight at the effrontery of the little man in the boat. Then, wistfully, they watch him fade into the distance. One crazy individual man has touched, for one exciting and then sad moment, the depths of their insulated lives in this world of the immaculate machine.

In other stories, Clark achieves more variations, turning his basic themes—as it were—through a prism. In "The Anonymous," an intellectual with three college degrees works to connect the world of Indian-school children with the "white" world that sponsors the school, only to find that the supreme failure comes not from Cuyler, the aggressively compromising director of the school, or from Jenny, the innocently wanton Indian maiden, but from Peter Carr, the "coffee-colored fake" (92), a dude-ranch Indian out to memorize enough parlor-room facts to qualify himself for marriage into the vapid world of money and manners.[9] In "The Fish Who Could Close His Eyes," primitive values are represented by a feebleminded misfit, caught in a surrealistic world of science where his fondest dreams are horribly crushed by scientific fact. In "The Indian Well" Clark writes a paradigmatic version of *The Track of the Cat*, but in "The Portable Phonograph" he turns his prism once more and writes of a primitive time in the future, after the Bomb has dropped, when man clings desperately to his last vestige of culture (a phonograph and a few classical records) and to his most ancient heritage, a club for protection. In these and in other stories, Clark describes the intimate presence of the primordial in the lives of men, regardless of geography or historical time.

"The Buck in the Hills," one of Clark's best short stories, illustrates this intimate presence. Significantly, the hero is undergoing a "clean, cold" (97), and Hemingwayish restoration of his tattered sensibilities. Much of the detail is pure Clark—the swim is naked, the hero sings in wordless ecstasy, "the peak was sacred," and "the climb was pilgrimage" (95)—but the style is frequently comparable to Hemingway's. The hero is doing what Jake Barnes and Bill Gorton are doing on their fishing trip in *The Sun Also Rises*. Clark's hero has lost contact with permanent meanings, and he has journeyed to his Walden to replenish his soul. The Hemingway *now*, the need to get it just right, to have nothing cheap or brutish disrupt the ceremony: these are the essentials of the restoration.

The hero's partner, however, intrudes on the ceremony with a sickening story. A third member of the party has deliberately crippled a deer and herded it eight miles back to camp in order to avoid having to carry it. The hero had wanted to hold to that sense of balance he was beginning to establish: "The story made a difference though, as if it were a lot darker all at once, and we were farther away from other people than before, and there were things alive in the rocks, watching us" (106). The next morning, when the two friends leave, the atmosphere is still antagonistic: "There was something listening behind each tree and rock we passed, and something waiting among the taller trees down slope, blue through the falling snow. They wouldn't stop us, but they didn't like us, either. The snow was their ally" (109). And there is, of course, no Christian justice in this ominous watching. There is, rather, the ancient curse of a people, with no attention paid to the rights of innocent individuals. Modern man's dismissal of archetypal and "unjust" watching, Clark feels, has cut him off from what *is*.

V *The Relevance of Walter Clark*

The ancient curse leveled on the people of the twentieth century, as portrayed by the reasoning of the practical hunter, is a bifurcating egoism. A long essay-story entitled "The Writer and the Professor: or, Where Is the Little Man Inside?" is an important study of the problem. The first half of the piece is comically autobiographical. Clark explains that he has accepted, with "cheerful and acquiescent imbecility," [10] an invitation to deliver a lecture as part of a summer course to be taught by Dr. S. I. Hayakawa. The style is mockingly academic as Clark jokes his own developing terror: he had thought he could get by with the usual meaningless professorial nonsense, but he is to speak, he discovers, as the writer. "My trepidation," he writes, "became unqualified panic" (65). He smokes cigarettes until the "smudge" blocks out the pages he is trying to read. He wonders desperately if he might "abandon abstract, technical formulative considerations" (65), but "the vacuous abstractions and generalizations [continue] to intrude with paralyzing effect" (66). The waste basket is filled, he takes to muttering to himself, and stilted thoughts come out: "The critical or revisional process, language values: denotational, connotational, contextual, creativity in the colleges" (66). Then phrases begin to come of their own accord, "The Three Little R's," and "Back to the Little Red Schoolhouse," culminating in "Teach the Little Bastards to Spell!" (66).

Clark is creating a joke on himself, but he is not mocking his own values, as the following passage makes clear:

Had not my inner crying out . . . suggested that . . . every child, in his spontaneous early endeavours at expression, recapitulates the artistic evolution of the race? And did not this recapitulation, since certainly all primitive art was essentially religious in source and intention, suggest in turn that even now the primary impulse of the arts was religious, ritualistic—their central hope, however much diluted by time and civilized detachment and irrelevant rationalization, the same old one of propitiating or enlisting Nature, the Gods, God, or whatever name one wishes to give to the encompassing and still mysterious whole, and of acting, as it were, as the shaman, the witch-doctor, the intermediary, between poor suffering man and the occult powers which control him? (72)

The primordial, to Clark, does not describe a time in the historical past; it describes the most fundamental nature of man. History does shape us, of course, and Clark the professor has fallen ironic victim to the twentieth-century curse he feared, apparently, all of his adult life. He is two people, the intellectually self-conscious professor and the unhousebroken writer; and there is no connection between the two. They live in separate houses, and both are severely damaged.

At this point, the essay shifts into story. The professor-half plots a way out of his dilemma. Unable to get away from meaningless academic generalizations, he will secretly plant a tape recorder in the backyard of the writer-self, near his favorite outdoor chair, leave and then reappear openly, lure him into conversation, and thus tap the writing-self for vital and concrete materials for the lecture. The story which follows is an elaborate comment on the Henry James problem and on the Walter Clark problem. The professor talks like a parody of a Henry James character; the writer bullies and mocks the professor, turning at times to the James style himself by way of further teasing. The creative process is analyzed (the writer must think through things; he cannot think through words), a good many writers are mentioned, and James is discussed in detail. Modern man, the writer keeps insisting, cannot escape his homunculus; and he cites Lambert Strether as the prime example. James's characters talk nonsense, but he knew they did: "James was a completely, invariably, and increasingly ironic man" (101). He realized his own limitations, "and they were very much those of Strether, the man who refused to engage in life directly, to risk the deep feeling or the major event . . ." (101). The story ends with one more ironic turn. The writer has known the tape recorder was there, and he has played professor, becoming, of all things, the learned literary critic. Their roles, the writer concludes, have become reversed: the wrong half has told the story, the wrong half has made the comment.

The bifurcation of the conscious self from the unconscious self and not the corruption of the frontier, I suggest, is the central concern of Walter Clark. Even Art in *The Track of the Cat* and certainly Tim in *The City of Trembling Leaves* and, most obviously, Davies in *The Ox-Bow Incident* are more troubled by a noxious intellectualism than by nostalgia for the "good old days." Clark's fiction, it seems to me, is disturbingly relevant to this time and to this nation. His belief that values must be evoked (not analyzed into a neat package) is in keeping with current efforts, many of them wild and hopeless, to recover some sense of meaning and vitality; and his belief that evil is in a state of being more than in conscious intentions is certainly relevant to current thinking.[11] Among numerous instances, the following, from James Baldwin's *The Fire Next Time*, seems especially pertinent: "I use the word 'love' here not merely in the personal sense but as a state of being, or a state of grace—not in the infantile American sense of being made happy but in the tough and universal sense of quest and daring and growth." [12]

Baldwin's ideas about the white man's tensions before integration are also strikingly relevant: "These tensions are rooted in the very same depths as those from which love springs, or murder. The white man's unadmitted—and apparently, to him, unspeakable—private fears and longings are projected onto the Negro. The only way he can be released from the Negro's tyrannical power over him is to consent, in effect, to become black himself, to become a part of that suffering and dancing country that he now watches wistfully from the heights of his lonely power and, armed with spiritual traveller's checks, visits surreptitiously after dark." [13]

Clark's explorations into the "unspeakable" may well represent one version of the only hope we have. Clearly, man cannot survive without a belief in love "as a state of being," without belief in something larger than himself; and scientistic reason has failed to produce the something larger. The literary endeavors of Walter Clark have produced no magic answers—not that any were promised—and the experience has apparently been disruptive; but Clark—one of those men bold enough to see that homunculus must be confronted—has already been where most of the rest of us have yet to go. We would do well to study his journey.

Notes and References

1. Letter to Max Westbrook, May 12, 1963.
2. Letter to Max Westbrook, September 11, 1963. Swallow makes essentially the same statement, further developed, in his "The Mavericks," *Critique*, II (Winter, 1959), 74–92.

Chapter One

1. *The Sacred and the Profane* (New York, 1961), p. 20.
2. *Ibid.*, 20–21.
3. For sacred man, a myth *is* the real; for profane man, a myth is at best an imaginative comment *about* the real. This distinction is fundamental to Clark and to the sacred tradition generally; see, for example, Bronislaw Malinowski, *Magic, Science and Religion* (New York, 1954), p. 108.
4. *The Sacred and the Profane,* p. 22.
5. See, for example, James K. Folsom, *The American Western Novel* (New Haven, 1966). Folsom's thesis about Cooper, however, works very well when applied to minor and nostalgic Western writers (see, especially, p. 55).
6. My chief source for these biographical comments is a letter from Clark, dated June 1, 1963, in which he responds in detail to a series of typical questions about his schooling, family, and career.
7. (M.A. thesis, Department of English, University of Nevada, 1931) p. II.
8. *Ibid.*, 20.
9. Written on the back of p. 3 of the June 1 letter cited above.
10. "A Study in Robinson Jeffers" (M.A. thesis, University of Vermont, 1934), n. 2, p. 21.
11. "The Writer and the Professor," *Chrysalis*, II (Spring, 1962), p. 83.
12. *Ibid.*, 83, with minor revisions by Clark on a copy he kindly presented to me.
13. "The Sword Singer," XXVI.
14. *Ibid.*, XXVII.

15. *Ibid.*, XXIX.

16. *Ibid.*, XXXI.

17. "A Study in Robinson Jeffers," 11.

18. *Ibid.*, 20.

19. *Ibid.*, 21.

20. *Ibid.*, 27.

21. From Part I of Section Four of "Psychological Aspects of the Mother Archetype," readily available in Violet Staub De Laszlo (ed.), *The Basic Writings of C. G. Jung* (New York, 1959), p. 345.

22. *Ibid.*, 344–45.

23. "A Study in Robinson Jeffers," 48.

24. *Ibid.*, 117.

25. *Ibid.*, 114.

26. See Part III of Swallow's "The Mavericks," cited above; and Wallace Stegner's "Born a Square: The Westerner's Dilemma," *Atlantic*, CCXIII (January, 1964), 46–50.

27. Quotations from Clark about his reading are from the June 1 letter cited above.

28. Clark played a significant and quietly courageous role in the struggle for academic freedom at the University of Nevada in the early 1950's. See *New York Times*, June 6, 1953, p. 19, col. 7; *Time*, LXI (June 15, 1953), 50; and *ibid.*, LXI (June 22, 1953), 43–44. Interesting also is Clark's place in the famous *Howl* trial. Mark Schorer was the principal witness for the defense, but Clark's presence as a witness and his brief, clear statement indicate his attitude toward prudish censorship. See David Perlman, "How Captain Hanrahan Made *Howl* a Best-Seller," *Reporter*, XVII (December 12, 1957), 37–39.

Chapter Two

1. For an interesting and informative presentation of the ideas and attitudes of Western novelists, see John R. Milton (ed.), "The Western Novel: A Symposium," *South Dakota Review*, II (Autumn, 1964), 3–36. The novelists interviewed are representative of those I refer to as central or intrinsic: Frederick Manfred, Frank Waters, Walter Van Tilburg Clark, Vardis Fisher, Harvey Fergusson, Forrester Blake, Paul Horgan, and Michael Straight.

2. *The City of Trembling Leaves* (New York, 1945), p. 14. Especially relevant also is Clark's discussion of the "nuclear"; see pp. 200 ff. in the same novel. The standard reference for Jung, of course, is "Archetypes of the Collective Unconscious."

3. I was impressed by the clarity and forcefulness of Mircea Eliade's explanation in his *Cosmos and History: The Myth of the Eternal*

Return (New York, 1959), p. 156. The chapter on "The Terror of History" is especially interesting.

4. For examples of reviewers who feel Clark's power and praise his narrative ability but who dislike and misread what makes him Western, see the following: Hamilton Basso, "The Great Open Spaces," *New Yorker,* XXV (June 4, 1949), 76, 79; Vernon Young, "An American Dream and Its Parody," *Arizona Quarterly,* VI (Summer, 1950), 112–23; Jean Garrigue, "The Watchful Gods and Other Stories," *New Republic,* CXXIII (December 25, 1950), 20.

5. Further difficulty, I realize, will be caused by the fact that for some readers I will seem to be talking about the values of Jean-Jacques Rousseau or Paul Gauguin or Jack Kerouac while stubbornly refusing to admit it. I can only hope that in the process of the book the differences will become clear. Basically, Clark does not advocate the escapist return to nature of Rousseau, the pure forms of Gauguin (who wished to close his eyes to what was in front of him in order to see the essence), or the anti-intellectualism of Kerouac. The best Western writers generally are neither nostalgic nor inspirationalist. Sacrality, I hope to show, is a good deal more tough-minded than what passes in the marketplace for practicality and realism.

6. John Steinbeck, *The Log From the Sea of Cortez* (New York, 1962), pp. 132–35. Steinbeck also agrees with Clark, D. H. Lawrence, and others that thought comes afterwards: "Only at the last when the move is mounted and prepared does thought place a roof on the building and bring in words to explain and to justify" (*The Winter of Our Discontent* [New York, 1961], p. 91).

7. See "The Writer and the Professor," *Chrysalis,* I (Spring, 1962), *passim.*

8. This point will also be discussed in the chapter on *The City of Trembling Leaves* (hero Tim Hazard is fascinated by Henry Adams) and in the concluding chapter. Note, also, the relevance of Davies in *The Ox-Bow Incident* and Art in *The Track of the Cat.*

9. See, for example, Jung's explanation of the authoritative voice of the unconscious in his *Psychology and Religion* (New Haven, 1938, 1963), p. 49. See also the first essay, "The Autonomy of the Unconscious Mind." An explanation from a different viewpoint is C. S. Lewis, *The Abolition of Man* (New York, 1947), especially chap. ii.

10. The following, from "Archetypes of the Collective Unconscious," is directly comparable to Clark's own thinking: "If we now try to cover our nakedness with the gorgeous trappings of the East, as the theosophists do, we would be playing our history false. A man does not sink down to beggary only to pose afterwards as an Indian potentate. It seems to me that it would be far better stoutly to avow

our spiritual poverty, our symbollessness, instead of feigning a legacy to which we are not the legitimate heirs at all. We are, surely, the rightful heirs of Christian symbolism, but somehow we have squandered this heritage. We have let the house our fathers built fall into decay, and now we try to break into Oriental palaces that our fathers never knew." Quoted from *The Basic Writings of C. G. Jung,* 298.

Chapter Three

1. See, for example, Ben Ray Redman, "Magnificent Incident," *Saturday Review of Literature,* XXIII (October 26, 1940), 6. Redman is representative in that his review is very favorable, with only minor reservations; but it contains no significant analysis. For the most part, he praises the tension in the novel, the suspense, Clark's abilities in craftsmanship. Essentially the same position is held, fifteen years later, by Jay Gurian, "The Unwritten West," *The American West,* II (Winter, 1965), 59–63. Clark is mentioned as one of a small number of Western artists who have begun to break from the stereotypes of escapist adventure stories. Still, the main praise for *The Ox-Bow Incident* is that the cavalry does not come to the rescue: "But for once in a western tale the characters interact toward an ironic, not a mechanically routine outcome" (61).

Typical of the general criticism on Clark is Chester E. Eisinger's essay in his *Fiction of the Forties* (Chicago, 1963). Eisinger writes that Clark has no interest in "society" or in "ideology" (310), but he describes *The Ox-Bow Incident* as a philosophical novel, as a "deliberate commingling of social and moral issues" (311). Eisinger's strategy is typical of much of the criticism of Clark's fiction: Clark is a transcendentalist; his novels do not constitute an accurate development of transcendentalism. Instead of concluding that it is therefore mistaken to call Clark a transcendentalist, Eisinger stubbornly pushes on to the astounding conclusion that Clark is therefore incoherent. Vernon Young does the same thing in his "Gods Without Heroes: The Tentative Myth of Van Tilburg Clark," *Arizona Quarterly,* VII (Summer, 1951), 110–19. Two critics I do not agree with, but whose positions and reasoning I respect and whose articles I recommend highly, are John Portz, "Idea and Symbol in Walter Van Tilburg Clark," *Accent,* XVII (Spring, 1957), 112–28; and Herbert Wilner, "Walter Van Tilburg Clark," *The Western Review,* XX (Winter, 1956), 103–22. Easily the best article on Clark, in my judgment, is John R. Milton's "The Western Attitude: Walter Van Tilburg Clark," *Critique,* II (Winter, 1959), 57–73.

2. *The Ox-Bow Incident* (New York, 1942), p. 4. Since this Readers Club edition seems the most readily available, I have used it for

the convenience of my readers. Subsequent references to this edition are cited parenthetically in the text.

3. "The very common prejudice against dreams is but one of the symptoms of a far more serious undervaluation of the human soul in general." See Jung's *Psychology and Religion*, 18.

4. *Ibid.*, 14.

5. *Ibid.*, 15.

6. *Ibid.*, 16.

7. Canby's attitude reminds one of Jake Barnes during the fishing scene in *The Sun Also Rises* when he wishes to keep Bill Gorton "going." The ritual drink with Canby is generally suggestive of Hemingway.

8. The role of the conscious mind in Clark is often that of an "internal monitor," a mode of rational reflection upon the feelings sensed by the unconscious. Curt, Art, and Hal of *The Track of the Cat*, Tim in *The City of Trembling Leaves*, and Buck in *The Watchful Gods* are just a few of the Clark characters who conduct an inner debate. Jung again is relevant: "As the archetypes, like all numinous contents, are relatively autonomous, they cannot be integrated simply by rational means, but require a dialectical procedure, a real coming to terms with them, often conducted by the patient in dialogue form, so that, without knowing it, he puts into effect the alchemical definition of the *meditatio:* 'an inner colloquy with one's good angel.'" See *The Basic Writings of C. G. Jung*, 325. See also, C. G. Jung and C. Kerenyi, *Essays on a Science of Mythology* (New York, 1949, 1963), p. 94.

9. Glenway Wescott's interests in and abilities with a primordial reality of the Wisconsin farmlands seems to have fallen into a type of decadence, but compare the following: "Stories like a series of question marks; questions which did not require an answer, questions at peace." See *The Grandmothers* (New York, 1927, 1955), p. 28.

10. Failure to see the presence of an archetypal reality in Clark leads to the mistaken conclusion that he is nostalgic or—in the case of *The Ox-Bow Incident*—naturalistic. See, for example, Loy Otis Banks, "The Credible Literary West," *The Colorado Quarterly*, VIII (Summer, 1959), 28–50. According to Banks, "the 'new' naturalism" is the "well-spring" of *The Ox-Bow Incident* (49). For an intelligent (there are useful explications of language patterns) but I think unsuccessful attempt (Swanson, a minor character, is given a major structural importance) to ground the novel in rational values, see Barclay W. Bates, "Clark's Man For All Seasons: The Achievement of Wholeness in *The Ox-Bow Incident*," *Western American Literature*, III (Spring, 1968), 37–49.

Chapter Four

1. See, for example, Lincoln Barnett, "Adventures of Timothy Hazard," *New York Times Book Review*, L (May 27, 1945), 4; Orville Prescott, "Outstanding Novels," *The Yale Review*, XXXV (September, 1945), 191–92; and Diana Trilling, "Fiction in Review," *The Nation*, CLX (June 23, 1945), 702–4. Clark has written to me (December 20, 1967) of an exception, a reviewer who *"had* seen what I was trying to do." The conclusion of this review, Clark felt, was a contradiction which had probably "been diplomatically appended by some apprehensive editor." But the substance of the review was excellent and "still, perhaps, trustworthy." The review, which is compatible with the position taken in this chapter, is by Charles Deneche, S.J., in *Best Sellers*, V (June 1, 1945), 45–46.

2. Letter to Max Westbrook, May 12, 1963.

3. I do not mean to suggest an "influence" so much as a Western interest in a kind of thing associated, academically, with the Haikai. Though I believe the interest to be prevalent even in long novels, it is easier to demonstrate in Western poetry. See, for example, Robert Bly's brief and fascinating "Dropping the Reader," an introduction to his *The Sea and the Honeycomb* (The Netherlands, 1966). Editor Bly has collected brief poems by various poets; the whole volume is interesting in its own right, though scarcely, for present purposes, Western.

More relevant is Bly's own poetry in, for example, *Silence in the Snowy Fields* (Middletown, 1953–62). Bly's ability to "drop the reader" with a brief and clear and moving experience—most obvious in a poem like "Watering the Horse"—has been developed into a cleanly disturbing technique. For an important study of how the Westerner's dedication to the specific has become part of his imagination, see James Wright (signed "Crunk"), "The Work of Gary Snyder," *The Sixties*, No. 6 (Spring, 1962), 25–42, especially 34–35.

4. Parenthetical page references to *The Track of the Cat* are to the Random House edition (New York, 1949).

5. See the three principles listed by Mircea Eliade, *Cosmos and History: The Myth of the Eternal Return*, 5–6.

6. Walter Van Tilburg Clark, *The City of Trembling Leaves* (New York, 1945), p. 3. Other references to this edition are cited parenthetically in the text.

7. *Cosmos and History*, 143.

8. *The Sacred and the Profane*, 116–21.

9. Edmund Wilson, "White Peaks and Limpid Lakes: A Novel About Nevada," *The New Yorker*, XXI (May 26, 1945), 75.

10. The traditional side of Clark's sacrality can be seen by reading

Arnold Van Gennep, *The Rites of Passage* (Chicago, 1960). See especially "The Territorial Passage" (pp. 15–25), in which many of the details (the lake as a natural boundary, the sacrilege of the stranger's entrance into a sacred place, the wavering between two worlds, the neutral zone, the purification of the ritual bath or swim, the guardians of the threshold, the offering of invocations) are directly comparable to details of the ritual mountain climb made by Tim and Rachel.

For one of the many differences between Clark's sacrality and that described in standard scholarly works, see *Cosmos and History*, 18. Eliade describes a separation between the sacred and the profane which is much too primitive, too unmodern for the world encountered by Walter Clark; Eliade's description of the primitive achievement also suggests a finality Clark believes to be no longer possible.

Chapter Five

1. Two essays by Wilson M. Hudson, though not written for the sake of comparing Freud to Jung, offer a remarkably clear and sound insight into the working of the minds of these two major psychologists: "Freud's Myth of the Primal Horde," *A Good Tale and a Bonnie Tune* (Dallas, 1964); "Jung on Myth and the Mythic," *The Sunny Slopes of Long Ago* (Dallas, 1966). Hudson's essay on Jung is especially relevant to the present study. For a brief statement of a basic difference between Freud and Jung, see C. G. Jung, *Psychology and Religion*, 30–31.

2. Joseph Campbell, *The Hero With a Thousand Faces* (New York, 1949, 1964), p. 15. Campbell's classic study of the hero is relevant, generally, to *The Track of the Cat* and *The City of Trembling Leaves*. His explanation of the "disoriented psyche" (60), for example, is directly relevant to the disorientation of Curt.

3. *Ibid.*, 30.

4. See, for example, the explanation of "breaking a taboo" and entering a "baneful zone" by Mircea Eliade, *Cosmos and History*, 97. Joseph Campbell (*The Hero With a Thousand Faces*, 51) suggests that the breaking of the taboo may not be an accident at all, may reveal a Freudian (suppressed) desire.

5. See, for example, *Cosmos and History*, 53. Sir James G. Frazer, *The Golden Bough*, of course, provides numerous other examples of the beast and of other standard motifs.

6. *Cosmos and History*, 57.

7. *Ibid.*, 97.

8. *Ibid.*, 98.

9. While Clark's themes are typically Western in important ways, his most characteristic strategy is the reverse of a pattern commonly associated with Western literature. The past (the primordial) is for

Clark a reality modern man cannot escape rather than a past modern man cannot return to. Compare, for example, the opening chapter of *The Track of the Cat* with the passage on "the primal beginning of the single cell in the slime" in Wallace Stegner, *The Big Rock Candy Mountain* (New York, 1957), p. 436.

10. Walter Van Tilburg Clark, *The Track of the Cat* (New York, 1949), p. 281. Further references to this edition are cited parenthetically in the text.

11. Jung explains that "anyone who descends into the unconscious gets into a suffocating atmosphere of egocentric subjectivity, and in this blind alley is exposed to the attack of all the ferocious beasts which the caverns of the psychic underworld are supposed to harbor. . . . Whoever goes to himself risks a confrontation with himself. . . . This confrontation is the first test of courage on the inner way, a test sufficient to frighten off most people, for the meeting with ourselves belongs to the more unpleasant things that can be avoided so long as we can project everything negative into the environment." *The Basic Writings of C. G. Jung*, 304.

12. Jung, again, makes a comparable statement: "For in actual reality we do not have at our command any power of cool reflection. . . . We are caught and entangled in aimless experience, and the judging intellect with its categories proves itself powerless." *Ibid.*, 316.

13. In Jungian terms, Curt is now possessed: *ibid.*, 323–24.

14. Traditionally characterized by a capacity for bewitching changes, as in Curt's dream, and by "an unbearable independence that does not seem at all proper in a psychic content": *ibid.*, 309, 310.

15. *Psychology and Religion*, 30–31.

16. *Ibid.*, 58.

Chapter Six

1. See Arthur Schilpp, "The Abdication of Philosophy," *The Texas Quarterly*, III (Summer, 1960), 1–20. Professor Schilpp's essay includes references to other excellent studies of cultural sell-out. Of special relevance is Alfred North Whitehead's analysis of "The Fallacy of the Perfect Dictionary," *Modes of Thought* (Cambridge, Eng., 1938), pp. 235 ff.

2. Typical are Ray B. West, Jr., "The Nature Stage," *Saturday Review of Literature*, XXXIII (September 30, 1950), 17–18; Harvey Swados, "Hawks and Men," *The Nation*, CLXXI (October 7, 1950), 317–18; and, for a longer study, Vernon Young, "Gods Without Heroes: The Tentative Myth of Van Tilburg Clark," *Arizona Quarterly*, VII (Summer, 1951), 110–19. West reviews *The Watchful Gods and Other Stories* sympathetically, but he feels that Clark has fallen shy, has not come through. Swados considers the title story a failure,

voicing the recurrent objection that Clark is not concerned with human beings. Young feels that for Clark, "Man . . . is usually . . . inarticulate, juvenile, somewhat priggish, given to chivalric and maudlin conceptions of Woman, but with a hawk's clear eye for the structure and movement of the wilderness" (110–11). Young, like Chester Eisinger, seems to assume that a writer advocates the qualities of his heroes even when those qualities are shown by the author to be the cause of crimes and failures and misunderstanding.

3. Walter Van Tilburg Clark, *The Watchful Gods and Other Stories* (New York, 1950), p. 200. Further references to this edition are indicated by parenthetical page numbers in the text.

4. A distrust of reason, with numerous exceptions of course, is characteristic of Western literature generally. The Westerner's belief in the primordial can lead to a belief in some modern form of tradition and thus to conservatism of one type or another, and thus to the emphasis on reason found, for example, in Yvor Winters. More characteristic, however, is an association of reason with the intellect, the intellectual, and therefore the bookish. Variations extend from the unrealistic and nostalgic "sixth sense" of the Hollywood and horse-opera hero to realistic and modern insights into unconscious thought found in Clark, Steinbeck, Manfred, and others. See my "The Themes of Western Fiction," *Southwest Review*, XLIII (Summer, 1958), 232–38.

Chapter Seven

1. *Ten Women in Gale's House and Shorter Poems* (Boston, 1932), p. 9. Further page-references are cited parenthetically.

2. An uncollected story, "Chuangtse and the Prince of the Golden Age" is available in *Western Review*, XIII (Winter, 1949), 87–97. The story is an allegorical spoof of abstract idealism. For a good example of Clark's fictive explorations of the haunting relation between man and animal, see "Trial at Arms," *Saturday Evening Post*, CCXIII (January 25, 1941), 14–15 ff. The relation, it should be pointed out, is not mystical; Clark's animals remain animals. The freezing comes from seeing eyes looking out of no-soul, eyes which—like the desert —reveal to man the watching unhumanness of his universe.

3. "Strength of Autumn End" and "Of the Broken Brotherhood," with a joint title, "Kindred," *Poetry*, XLIII (November, 1933), 70, 71; "Hook" is included in *The Watchful Gods and Other Stories;* "The Rise and the Passing of Bar," uncollected, was published in *The Virginia Quarterly Review*, XIX (Winter, 1943), 80–96.

4. See for example, his *Folk Laughter on the American Frontier* (New York, 1949). Perhaps the best guide to the pioneering scholarship of Boatright and others is still J. Frank Dobie, *Guide to Life and*

Literature of the Southwest (Dallas, 1942–52). In addition to standard bibliographical sources for American literature in general, the recent special bibliographies in *South Dakota Review* and *Western American Literature* are very useful.

5. See Dobie's Introduction to his *The Mustangs* (New York, 1934–54).

6. Fundamental to this change is the influence of land in Clark's thinking. "The desert," he writes, "does not move either. It does not stir or make a sound. It has no rhythm but the visible, static rhythm of its shapes. So, altogether, it is more complete, more remote, more appallingly indifferent than ocean is to the nagging, necessary little human sense of self-importance. . . . This [Nevada] is a region of extremes, but of extremes that exist at the same time, of extremes not very far apart, yet quite separate." See "Nevada's Fateful Desert," *Holiday*, XXII (November, 1957), 77, 103.

7. "The Wind and the Snow of Winter" might seem an exception; what has been lost, however, are old cronies and old times, not a pure and unsettled nature. "The Rise and the Passing of Bar," like the better known "Hook," is in my reading a story of powers found most uncluttered in an animal outside and perhaps prior to civilization; but Clark does not associate such powers with the historical past. The energy which drives Bar to fight is the energy which drives the lynch mob in *The Ox-Bow Incident*, the energy which breaks out in distortion and sends Curt running to his death in *The Track of the Cat*.

8. *The Watchful Gods and Other Stories*, 16, 22. Further references to this edition are cited parenthetically in the text.

9. Perhaps the best known novel on the subject is Oliver La Farge, *Laughing Boy* (Boston, 1929). The novel, which still makes good reading, includes direct parallels to Clark. La Farge writes, for example, of an evil which makes tracks, which can follow you (34), an evil which has the autonomous quality described by Clark, Eliade, Jung, and others. La Farge also has an appreciation of the hitting power of brief imagery and of the capacity of American education to dull one's ear to this power (160). One of the best novels I have seen on the subject is Frank Waters, *The Man Who Killed the Deer* (New York, 1942). For passages especially relevant to Clark see pp. 14, 46, 76, 77, 91, 115–16, and 194.

10. Walter Van Tilburg Clark, "The Writer and the Professor, or, Where Is the Little Man Inside?" *Chrysalis*, II (Spring, 1962), 60–107, quotation from p. 64. References, hereafter cited parenthetically in the text, are from my copy, in which Clark has made a few emendations.

11. Jewish novelists like Saul Bellow and Bernard Malamud, for example, are more concerned with being and with contemporary

touches of archetypal realities than with the isolated intentions of the conscious will. See the corrective review of William J. Handy, "Malamud's *The Fixer:* Another Look," *Northwest Review,* VIII (Spring, 1967), 74–82. The best work of the Beats is also relevant, Lawrence Ferlinghetti's *A Coney Island of the Mind,* for example. I do not, of course, refer to the work of writers like Henry Miller who exploit the primordial in us all as a means of buggy-whipping whatever Puritan hopes yet remain alive.

12. James Baldwin, *The Fire Next Time* (New York, 1962–64), p. 128. The Reverend Osgood, in *The Ox-Bow Incident,* and Curt, in *The Track of the Cat,* are about as moral, in the sense of immediate intentions, as the crisis will permit them to be; both fail, in Baldwin's terms, because their "state of being" is a personal quicksand, not a proper foundation for moral action.

13. *Ibid.,* 129. Space limitations preclude development here, but much of our modern social protest is directly related to the general feeling that we can work our way out of the wasteland only by facing honestly the personal archetypes of the human experience.

Selected Bibliography

The bibliography which follows should be supplemented by John R. Kuehl's "Walter Van Tilburg Clark: A Bibliography," *Bulletin of Bibliography*, XXII (September-December, 1956), 18–20; and by Richard Etulain's "Walter Van Tilburg Clark: A Bibliography," *South Dakota Review*, III (Autumn, 1965), 73–77. Kuehl includes several items (primarily reviews and reprints in anthologies) not listed by Etulain or in my bibliography. Etulain's more recent study brings the Clark bibliography up to date. The following compilation is greatly indebted to both.

Clark's letters are important, but they have not been published; and, out of respect for the author's wishes, they are not now available for study. The late Alan Swallow wrote me that his correspondence with Clark, although not steady, extended over a twenty-year period, beginning in the early 1940's with discussions of Clark's developing craftsmanship. Other important letters are scattered but—so far as I am aware of them—could be located by the usual procedures.

As Etulain indicates, manuscript copies of *The Ox-Bow Incident* and *The Track of the Cat* are at the Library of Congress, while the University of Nevada Library holds a manuscript of *The Watchful Gods*. The Library of Congress also holds an important draft of an early version of the beginning of *The City of Trembling Leaves*.

PRIMARY SOURCES

1. *Poems*
Ten Women in Gale's House and Shorter Poems. Boston: The Christopher Publishing House, 1932. The title poem is commented on briefly in Chapter 7. Among the more significant of the shorter poems are "The Wooing of Harlequin," for its suggestion of a possible relation between Clark and Wallace Stevens ("Harlequin sat in the blue of the moon/Plucking his sweet guitar"); "Dwight Marlowe," for a possible relation between Clark and Edgar Lee Masters; and "In Fear of Spring," for—the best of all reasons—its being a fine poem.
Three of Clark's best poems are not collected: "Strength of Autumn

End" and "Of the Broken Brotherhood," with a common title of "Kindred," *Poetry,* XLIII (November, 1933), 70, 71; and "Love as of Hawks," *ibid.,* XLIV (September, 1934), 311.

Other poems, not discussed in the present study because of lack of space, may be listed as follows:

"Big Dusk," *Troubador,* IV (Autumn, 1932), 9.

"Blue Alley Corner," *Winnowings from the Mill,* VI (March, 1933), 16–18.

Christmas Comes to Hjalsen, Reno. Reno: Reno Publishing Company, 1930.

"Communion with the Inheritor," *Winnowings from the Mill,* VI (May, 1933), 63.

"Cubist City Quatrains," *ibid.,* VII (March, 1934), 11–12.

"Dawn—Washoe Valley," *Troubador,* IV (Autumn, 1932), 9.

"The Hounds of Finn," *American Poetry Journal,* XIII (February, 1935), 14–15.

"Momentary," *Winnowings from the Mill,* VII (May, 1934), 15.

"The Ox-Team," *ibid.,* VI (March, 1933), 29.

"Pigeons in the Park," *ibid.,* VI (May, 1933), 21.

"Pyramid Lake," *Troubador,* IV (Autumn, 1932), 25.

"The Third One," *Winnowings from the Mill,* VII (December, 1933), 21–22.

"To Ease Waiting," *ibid.,* VII (May, 1934), 2.

"To a Friend with New Shoes," *ibid.,* VIII (November, 1934), 23.

2. *Books of Fiction*

Clark has published four volumes of fiction. In order of publication, they are as follows:

The Ox-Bow Incident. New York: Random House, 1940.

The City of Trembling Leaves. New York: Random House, 1945.

The Track of the Cat. New York: Random House, 1949.

The Watchful Gods and Other Stories. New York: Random House, 1950.

Each of the four volumes was published simultaneously in Toronto, Canada. All four have been published in paperback, but a catalogue listing and a copy in hand, as all college instructors know, is no guarantee that a paperback is available. Hiding behind the past tense, then, *The City of Trembling Leaves* has been published by Popular Library; *The Ox-Bow Incident,* by Vintage; and *The Ox-Bow Incident, The Track of the Cat,* and *The Watchful Gods and Other Stories* by Signet. Clark's chief publisher in England has been Victor Gollancz, Limited. John R. Keuhl, in his bibliography of Clark, reports that the first half of *The City of Trembling Leaves* was published as *Tim Hazard* by William Kimber and Company (London, 1951).

Significant introductions, all for *The Ox-Bow Incident,* are as follows: Clifton Fadiman's journalistic introduction to The Readers Club edition (New York, 1942); Walter Prescott Webb's folksy afterword for the Signet edition (New York, 1960); and Clark's own introduction to the *Time* edition (New York, 1962), which includes also a sane, informal foreword by unnamed *Time* editors. Clark's comments are honest and helpful, pointing out, briefly, the strength of the novel and the one major weakness (it explains itself too overtly).

The title story of *The Watchful Gods and Other Stories* was previously unpublished. The other stories were first published as follows:

"Hook," *Atlantic Monthly,* CLXVI (August, 1940), 223–34.

"The Wind and the Snow of Winter," *Yale Review,* XXXIV (December, 1944), 227–40.

"The Rapids," *Accent,* I (Winter, 1941), 76–81.

"The Anonymous," *Virginia Quarterly Review,* XVII (Summer, 1941), 349–69.

"The Buck in the Hills," *Rocky Mountain Review,* VII (Spring-Summer, 1943), 1 ff.

"Why Don't You Look Where You're Going?" *Accent* I (Summer, 1941), 195–99.

"The Indian Well," *ibid.,* III (Spring, 1943), 131–43.

"The Fish Who Could Close His Eyes," *Tomorrow,* V (February, 1946), 9–16.

"The Portable Phonograph," *The Yale Review,* XXXI (September, 1941), 53–60.

3. *Short Stories Not Collected in* The Watchful Gods and Other Stories

"The Ascent of Ariel Goodbody," *The Yale Review,* XXXII (Winter, 1943), 337–49. Directly comparable to the farcical ironies of the Carmel section (especially Chapter 48 on Knute Fenderson) of *The City of Trembling Leaves,* an aspect of Clark's technique that needs further study.

"Chuangtse and the Prince of the Golden Age," *The Western Review,* XIII (Winter, 1949), 87–97. An allegorical spoof of idealism.

"A Letter to the Living," *The Nation,* CLIV (June 13, 1942), 679–82. Quietly powerful, perhaps the best of the uncollected stories. Would be a good place to begin the needed study of the relation between Clark and Hemingway. See, for example, the paragraph beginning "The bird killed cleanly" (680), which is almost pure Hemingway. The sense of living or dying or killing cleanly which we associate with Hemingway is here combined with the sense of the primordial found throughout Clark.

"Personal Interview," *The New Yorker,* XVIII (December 12, 1942), 23–26. Short story using the monologue technique. A high school football coach, after four winning seasons, has accepted a job coaching football at State and is being interviewed. The interviewer's questions and moral tone are clear to the reader, though we read only the answers of the coach. With "gutsy" honesty, the coach never sees the moral point, reveals himself as a hypocrite who "uses" his players to win. The style reminds one of "You know Me, Al," though the story is basically serious. A successful but not a major story.

"Prestige," *Saturday Evening Post,* CCXIII (April 19, 1941), 14 ff. A trick of viewpoint, possibly the only slick story Clark has submitted for publication.

"The Pretender," *The Atlantic,* CLXI (April, 1942), 482–91. A minor effort on a theme comparable to the one brilliantly developed in the portrait of Curt in *The Track of the Cat.*

"The Rise and the Passing of Bar," *Virginia Quarterly Review,* XIX (Winter, 1943), 80–96. One of the best of the stories not collected in *The Watchful Gods.* Bar is a wild stallion that becomes the leader of his herd and finally falls. The story is directly comparable in almost every way to "Hawk"; it is, in my judgment, an even finer story.

"Trial at Arms," *Saturday Evening Post,* CCXIII (January 25, 1941), 14–15 ff. A successful story of a boy's first kill; significant also as part of Clark's long interest in the empathy between man and animal.

4. *Other Primary Sources*

"Emigrants on the Oregon Trail," *Saturday Review of Literature,* XXXII (October 8, 1949), 21–22. Review of A. B. Guthrie, Jr.'s *The Way West.* A favorable and perceptive review. Discusses Guthrie's growth since *The Big Sky.* Significant instance of Clark's concern with structure, a concern which characterizes his reviews.

"The Ghost of an Apprehension," *The Pacific Spectator,* III (Summer, 1949), 254–63. Clark recounts an instance of his own creative process. He selects "The Portable Phonograph" because "it was more than ordinarily conscious in its inception" (254), an understandable reason, but one which makes the essay largely foreign to an understanding of Clark's more "ordinary" and less conscious creative process.

"Important Authors of the Fall, Speaking for Themselves," *New York Herald Tribune,* XXVII (October 8, 1950), 18. Several authors of recent books write brief comments on their lives, careers, hobbies, work habits, plans. Clark mentions some of the places he has lived, comments on his reading, and—most importantly—reveals his feeling that all three of his novels and "Hook," "The

Portable Phonograph," "The Indian Well," and "The Wind and the Snow of Winter" are *one* story.

"Introduction." *The Big Sky.* New York: Time Books Incorporated, 1964. Describes the popular myth of the unrealistic cowboy hero in contrast with the more truly heroic but almost forgotten mountain man. Concludes that only heroes "born in verity can give a nation a soul" (xvi).

"Introduction." *The Ox-Bow Incident.* New York: Time Books Incorporated, 1962. A revealing insight into the artist's mind which, like "The Ghost of an Apprehension," Clark later regretted having written.

"Nevada's Fateful Desert," *Holiday,* XXII (November, 1957), 76 ff. Important for an understanding of Clark. Descriptions of land (specifically desert and mountain) lead to an acute analysis of the psychological and religious meanings of man's relation to nature.

"Reno: The City State" in *Rocky Mountain Cities,* ed. RAY B. WEST. New York: W. W. Norton and Company, Inc., 1949. Interesting in its own right as a good prose account of Reno, but relevant also are the suggestion that "Council Rock" (34) was known to ancient Indians (for a possible comparison to "Cathedral Rock" in *The Track of the Cat*), the further evidence (34) of Clark's familiarity with Fremont's expeditions (whose journals suggest that Joe Sam's memory is not the illusion Curt thinks it is), and for brief background information relevant to *The City of Trembling Leaves* (the context of Mr. Hazard's heroic defense of Willis [43], the description of Sunday outings like those of the Hazard and Turner families as typical of Reno life [52]). The final paragraph—with its description of having the state "literally"—is a clear example of Clark's sacrality. The land is absorbed physically, not symbolically.

"A Spark to Breathe On," *New Republic,* CXXVI (February, 1952), 18–19. Review of Erich Maria Remarque's *Spark of Life* (translated by James Stern). An intelligent review, with sound reasons given for favorable and unfavorable comments. Includes evidence of Clark's belief that a realistic affirmation is much needed and is *real* (see especially the last paragraph of the review).

"A Study in Robinson Jeffers." M.A. thesis, University of Vermont, 1934. General study of Jeffers with brief attention to his life, several comparisons of Jeffers with other poets, a chapter on Jeffers' ideas, brief studies of influences, and some close analysis.

"Sword Singer: The Tale of Tristram Retold: With an Introductory Essay Concerning Sources of the Tristram Legend." M.A. thesis,

University of Nevada, 1931. The introductory essay is 47 pages long; Clark's original version of the tale, in verse, is 136-pages long.

"The Teaching and Study of Writing," *Western Review,* XIV (Spring, 1950), 169–74. Clark's answers to typical questions about writing. Useful both for the intelligence of the answers given and for the insight provided into Clark's feelings about the relation of a writer to his materials.

"A Timely Coming: WR and RW," *Contact,* I (1959), 49–53. Sketches the history of the *Intermountain Review of English and Speech* which became the *Rocky Mountain Review,* then the *Western Review* and, currently, *Contact.* "RW" is Ray B. West, chief founder and editor, especially in the earlier stages when the West had almost no journals or quarterlies of literary quality.

"The Western Novel: A Symposium," ed. JOHN R. MILTON. *South Dakota Review,* II (Autumn, 1946), 3–36. Eight Western novelists give their answers to ten basic questions. The interview with Clark (17–19) is brief but significant.

"Windmills South of the Border," *Book Week,* II (September 27, 1964), 3, 23. Review of Robert Lewis Taylor's *Two Roads to Guadalupe.* Clark shows sympathy and understanding for an approach quite different from his own.

"The Writer and the Professor: or, Where Is the Little Man Inside?" *Chrysalis,* II (Spring, 1962), 60–107. Long essay-story which reveals in serio-comic fashion the price of being a self-conscious American responsible to both the intellectual present and the primordial past, a price paid by American artists from Hawthorne through Henry James to Walter Clark.

SECONDARY SOURCES

————. "Smothered Incident," *Time,* LIII (June 6, 1949), 104, 106. Review of *The Track of the Cat.* Typical of reviews which see no structural connection between Curt's hunt and the story back at the ranch house. Tries to read archetypal realities as symbols of a conscious realism, concludes that "a simple tale" of good and evil is "smothered in a stew of inarticulated meanings" (106).

BARNETT, LINCOLN. "Adventures of Timothy Hazard," *The New York Times Book Review,* L (May 27, 1945), 4. Review of *The City of Trembling Leaves.* Typical of reviewers who expected Clark's second novel to be like his first, found that it was not, and were disappointed. Typical also in assuming that *The City of Trembling Leaves* must be a "first" novel.

BLUESTONE, GEORGE. *Novels Into Film.* Baltimore: Johns Hopkins Press, 1957. Includes a chapter on *The Ox-Bow Incident,* a major study. Analyzes the novel, the film, and changes between the two, and comments on Clark's values generally. Quotes an important passage in a letter from Clark to Bluestone, but concludes, erroneously I think, that Clark has advocated a combination of Darwinism and Christianity. Still, an intelligent and rewarding study. Footnotes guide the reader to a dozen brief but significant comments on the film not listed in any other source.

BRACHER, FREDERICK. "California's Literary Regionalism," *American Quarterly* VII (Fall, 1955), 275–84. Worthwhile article on California regionalism, with special attention to Steinbeck, Saroyan, and Clark. Demonstrates convincingly that geography cannot be the basis for a definition; describes a quality of writing with geographical associations.

BROSSARD, CHANDLER. "Noble Hawks and Neurotic Women," *New American Mercury*, LXXII (February, 1951), 230–34. Review of *The Watchful Gods and Other Stories* (and Mary McCarthy's *Cast a Cold Eye*). High praise for Clark, though title story ignored. Brossard feels his own "vestigial memories" stirred (232), an interesting response in view of the fact that his approach is that of the intelligent reader and not that of the sophisticated critic armed with preconceptions.

CARPENTER, FREDERIC I. "The West of Walter Van Tilburg Clark," *College English*, XIII (February, 1952), 243–48. General article based on thorough reading of Clark. Contains many interesting suggestions (Clark's latent intellectualism and the importance of the chapter titles in *The City of Trembling Leaves*, for example), but none, unfortunately, are developed. (Also available in *The English Journal*, XLI [February, 1952], 64–69.)

DEVOTO, BERNARD. "Tame Indian, Lone Sailor," *The New York Times Book Review*, LV (September 24, 1950), 9, 18. Review of *The Watchful Gods and Other Stories*. Likes "Why Don't You Look Where You're Going?," "The Anonymous," and "The Buck in the Hills," but thinks the rest are pretentious, "a demonstration of what happens when arty writing moves into the Western landscape" (18). Title story is harshly attacked and "Hook" is called "low-grade Western mysticism" (18). Failing to see the sacrality in Clark, DeVoto also fails to see humor, irony, structural discipline.

EISINGER, CHESTER E. *Fiction of the Forties*. Chicago: University of Chicago Press, 1963. Argues that Clark is a transcendentalist and a monist, that transcendentalism is a desire to merge the self with the all and lose consciousness of the self, that Clark is interested in maturation and consequently in the development of the self, that Clark is therefore incoherent (315, 322–24). An example of criticism which employs predetermined categories to hunt for messages.

FOLSOM, JAMES K. *The American Western Novel*. New Haven: College and University Press, 1966. Argues unconvincingly that Western novels, even when stereotyped and unrealistic, carry the literary qualities of myth. Central thesis is that "whether the coming of civilization is good or ill is the burden of Western fiction" (31). Calls *The Ox-Bow Incident* a "parable of the posse which, though acting from the highest motives nevertheless does the worst possible thing" (123). The motives, however, are despicable. Analysis of *The Track of the Cat* culminates in the statement that Curt "cannot cope with the idea of a metaphysical evil principle, and when such a principle is inadvertently forced upon him he goes mad" (174). Curt, however, is clearly responsible for his own black painter.

FULLER, EDMUND. "Man Against Relentless Evil," *Saturday Review of Literature*, XXXII (June 4, 1949), 9–10. Review of *The Track of the Cat*. Includes a brief but interesting note, signed R. G., with suggestive background information about the composition of *The Track of the Cat* and Clark's attitudes toward his writing. Review raises the ghost of Clifton Fadiman's famous remark that Clark's first novel seemed to preclude further growth, makes the usual guess that *The City of Trembling Leaves* was written first and is highly autobiographical. Fuller holds that Art, in a sense, has "overcome the world" and that, if "there is any triumph in the book, it is his" (10). A favorable review, with a jolly attitude toward criticism: says you can take the novel as mystical if you want to, or just enjoy the story.

HILTON, JAMES. "Old, Nameless Terror in the High Sierras," *New York Herald Tribune Weekly Book Review*, XXV (June 5, 1949), 5. Review of *The Track of the Cat*. An example of a reviewer who places Clark in the right context and therefore thinks more highly of his novels. Says Clark touches "a deep spring of racial experience." Includes no significant analysis, does have some reservations, but offers high praise for the writer and the novel.

LEE, L. L. "Walter Van Tilburg Clark's Ambiguous American Dream," *College English*, XXVI (February, 1965), 382–87. Consistently intelligent and frequently brilliant; brief but major article. The sensitivity and the judgments are flawless.

MILTON, JOHN R. "The American Novel: The Search for Home, Tradition, and Identity," *Western Humanities Review*, XVI (Spring, 1962), 169–80. Important, general article on themes indicated by the title. Examples from Fitzgerald, Cooper, Steinbeck, Manfred, Fisher, and Clark (*The Track of the Cat*). Milton's thesis could profitably be applied to a study of—among others—*The City of Trembling Leaves*.

————. "The Western Attitude: Walter Van Tilburg Clark," *Critique*, II (Winter, 1959), 57–73. Best article on Clark yet written. Analyzes Clark's major works in the context of the West and its relation to the whole country. Coverage is excellent; analytical support, convincing. Milton is one of the finest scholars and critics writing in this field, and his work should be consulted by anyone interested in Western literature.

PICKREL, PAUL. "Outstanding Novels," *The Yale Review*, XXXIX (Autumn, 1949), 189–92. Reviews, among other recent novels, *The Track of the Cat*. Places Clark in the tradition of Hawthorne and Melville. Praises the writing but concludes that Clark does not "deal adequately" with the "ambiguities inherent in the situation" (191).

PORTZ, JOHN. "Idea and Symbol in Walter Van Tilburg Clark," *Accent*, XVII (Spring, 1957), 112–28. Major study. Reveals a thorough, highly intelligent reading of Clark. Emphasizes, quite rightly, the importance of unity and disunity, the relevance of intuitive apprehension. Portz supports his position by specific and sensitive analysis of the major works.

REDMAN, BEN RAY. "Magnificent Incident," *Saturday Review of Literature*, XXIII (October 26, 1940), 6. Review of *The Ox-Bow Incident*. High praise, with only slight reservations. Concentrates on plot summary, thinks Davies not successfully drawn, but finds the tension powerful and raises several points worth consideration.

RICE, JENNINGS. "A Life's Awakening to Music," *New York Herald Tribune Weekly Book Review*, XXI (May 27, 1945), 4. Review of *The City of Trembling Leaves*. Sensitive, favorable review. Rather than looking at critical preconceptions, Rice looks at the novel; the result is a perceptive and intelligent account, a rare exception among many mis-reviewers.

SANDOZ, MARI. "The Atlantic Bookshelf," *The Atlantic*, CLXXVI (July, 1945), 130. Review of *The City of Trembling Leaves*. Describes briefly what happens in the novel and then concludes: "This is a fine novel, a little overlong and wordy in spots, but so was young Timmy when self-conscious, and he was forgiven" (130). Favorable review but without supporting analysis.

SCHORER, MARK. "An Eloquent Novel of 'Place,'" *The New York Times Book Review*, LIV (June 5, 1949), 1, 16. Review of *The Track of the Cat*. Offers very high praise. Novel said to be "one of the great American novels of 'place'" (1), one which "may well be the achievement that twentieth-century American regionalism has needed to justify itself" (1). Schorer does not see the novel as metaphysical, however; the cat "is only real in dreams" (1).

STEGNER, WALLACE. "Born a Square: The Westerner's Dilemma," *The Atlantic,* CCXIII (January, 1964), 46–50. Provocative suggestions about the effect of Western guiltlessness (contra the South) on Western writing.

SWALLOW, ALAN. "The Mavericks," *Critique,* II (Winter, 1959), 74–92. Important general essay. Illustrates the continuing concern of the Westerner about lack of acceptance in the East. Holds that "the typical western story has at least two virtues," first, a simplicity which Swallow relates to Empson's definition of "pastoral" and, second, a capacity to "translate its themes into action" (84). Includes Swallow's explanation of why Clark is not writing: he is a perfectionist, and he has become too conscious of critical terms and methods.

TRILLING, DIANA. "Fiction in Review," *The Nation,* CLX (June 23, 1945), 702–4. Review of *The City of Trembling Leaves.* Disappointed that the novel is not as tight as *The Ox-Bow Incident,* believes *The City of Trembling Leaves* was probably written before *The Ox-Bow Incident,* and yet confesses that she has never read *The Ox-Bow Incident.* Finds "little virtue" in *The City of Trembling Leaves* (703) because it tries to be non-rational. Instance of a reviewer who assumes that rational knowledge is the only kind of knowledge, who judges any other approach by its worst examples, and who feels that sophisticated people need not read regional books in order to be able to judge them. A good example of the condescension which has angered many Western writers.

WEST, RAY B. "The Nature Stage," *Saturday Review of Literature,* XXXIII (September 30, 1950), 17–18. Reviews *The Watchful Gods and Other Stories.* Lacks supporting analysis, but sensitive, interesting. Compares Clark with others at a similar stage in their career, draws, with reservations, a generally favorable conclusion.

WILNER, HERBERT. "Walter Van Tilburg Clark," *The Western Review,* XX (Winter, 1956), 103–22. General and important study. Shows respect for Clark's writing, but holds that he fails, basically, in his characterizations. Intelligent study, good to read in conjunction with my own quite different conclusions. The comparison, for example, would invite much-needed study of the techniques of characterization associated with Western values.

WILSON, EDMUND. "White Peaks and Limpid Lakes: A Novel About Nevada," *The New Yorker,* XXI (May 26, 1945), 75–77. Typical misreview of *The City of Trembling Leaves.* Admits that Clark writes well, but fails to see any unity or selectivity in the novel. Concludes that Eastern taste is formed; Western taste, vital but uncontrolled.

YOUNG, VERNON. "Gods Without Heroes: The Tentative Myth of Van Tilburg Clark," *Arizona Quarterly*, VII (Summer, 1951), 110–19. General study of Clark. Assumes that each protagonist represents allegorically Clark's views of ultimate reality, finds that sensitive children and vicious adults do not represent the same thing, concludes that Clark's vision does not cohere. To sustain this approach through a reading of "The Buck in the Hills" concentrates on a character who never appears on stage and ignores the two characters who do appear. Concludes that Clark is good with landscape but not with characters. Argues that small boys and tennis are immature, that murder of a woman is mature. Says that permanent art cannot be written about a small town.

Index